THE PUPPY OF YOUR DREAMS IN 5 STEPS:

EVERYTHING YOU NEED TO KNOW ABOUT RAISING AN OBEDIENT DOG

KORY BAKER

The content contained within this book may not be reproduced, duplicated or transmitted without direct written permission from the author or the publisher.

Under no circumstances will any blame or legal responsibility be held against the publisher, or author, for any damages, reparation, or monetary loss due to the information contained within this book. Either directly or indirectly. You are responsible for your own choices, actions, and results.

Legal Notice:

This book is copyright protected. This book is only for personal use. You cannot amend, distribute, sell, use, quote or paraphrase any part, or the content within this book, without the consent of the author or publisher.

Disclaimer Notice:

Please note the information contained within this document is for educational and entertainment purposes only. All effort has been executed to present accurate, up to date, and reliable, complete information. No warranties of any kind are declared or implied. Readers acknowledge that the author is not engaging in the rendering of legal, financial, medical or professional advice. The content within this book has been derived from various sources. Please consult a licensed professional before attempting any techniques outlined in this book.

By reading this document, the reader agrees that under no circumstances is the author responsible for any losses, direct or indirect, which are incurred as a result of the use of the information contained within this document, including, but not limited to, — errors, omissions, or inaccuracies.

TABLE OF CONTENTS

INTRODUCTION

The idea of owning a dog is exciting for a lot of people. Yet training a puppy is where things typically begin to become stressful!

Dogs are a bundle of mixed feelings. On the one hand, there's the cute human-canine bond you feel when he cuddles you or sleeps on your feet. But on the other hand, there's the blend of shouting, cleaning, running, and patience it requires to actually train a puppy successfully.

It can be an arduous task when you try to control your dog or get him (or her) to obey your instructions. In fact, there's nothing as magical as telling a dog to "stay," and it stays. But I won't give you false hopes - dogs aren't born that way.

As with human babies, puppies need guidance and training. And this book delivers all that you need to do this successfully!

Specifically, I've provided in-depth strategies and cues on how you can get your dog from growling-puppy to loving-doggy. I know you came here for answers in this book. This step-by-step guide is based on my decades of experience training multiple dog breeds to help devoted dog owners just like you to raise an obedient dog.

If you're also a lover of dog tricks, or you're looking for practical ways to teach your dogs some cool tricks, then you've also picked up the right book. However, it begins with a basic understanding of obedience. They all work hand-in-hand.

You see, puppies start learning from birth, and good breeders begin handling and socializing right away. It's possible to start training the puppy as soon as it opens its eyes and walks. Despite their incapacity to concentrate for long periods, puppies learn simple obedience commands such as "sit," "down," and "stay" from a young age.

I know this because I've been training for over two decades now. I totally love dogs! Likewise, the cool part is that they seem to love me, too!

My passion for dogs made me pursue a career as a professional dog trainer, where I interacted with hundreds of dog owners like you from time to time. And trust me, I've had my fair share of dog disobedience. I once owned a German Shepard, Light Speed. That dog was one hard nut to crack!

Screaming and punishing your dog will only get you more frustrated as a dog owner. Trust me, I tried. 'Think like a dog' if you want your dog to listen to you. You need to understand that a puppy is like a human baby - young, naive, and incapable of grasping even the most basic instructions. Unless, of course, you employ a good strategy and a cool head when exercising patience, a key tactic.

Over the last decade, I've further gained on-the-ground experience and developed science-based strategies on the best ways to raise the perfect dog. I've applied these strategies to Light Speed and tons of other "hard dogs," and the results have been tremendous.

I can't make you any promises. But this I can say - although dogs are different, they're all wired the same. Various dog breeds, ages, and origins have been tested and perfected by the principles and strategies. With what I've outlined in this book, you'll soon be able to put an end to your dog problems in no time!

I've also summarized some really cool tricks that you can teach your canine friend. It's about to get fun!

Trust me; you don't want to postpone reading this. Training your dog early will benefit both of you. You want an easy dog-training life, so here's how to go about it.

So, are you ready to train your dog?

Training your dog can seem overwhelming at first, especially if you're a beginner. In reality, training a dog can be a very big undertaking. Frustrating, I might add.

So taking it step by step will make the overall process easier to handle. So, are you ready to go on this journey with me?

LET'S DO IT!

PART 1

PREPARING FOR YOUR PUP'S UPBRINGING.

CHAPTER 1

How to Raise a Puppy: Everything You Need to Know

I'll state it exactly as it is - raising a puppy isn't an easy task.

Sure, you must have seen tons of dog trainers exercising so much control over their dogs' behaviors. Or you've been to a dog obstacle course competition, so you presume that owning your puppy will be easy peasy. Well, not really!

Raising a dog can be fun, exciting, and frustrating at the same time. But with the right understanding that I've shared in this book and the correct mentality, I'm sure you'll scale through just fine.

But, it all begins with the acceptance that raising a puppy is an actual full-time responsibility. So, you should treat it accordingly.

This chapter describes everything you need to know about raising a puppy. After reading, you'll understand what kind of responsibility it is and whether or not you're ready to raise a puppy.

Let's dig in!

Raising a puppy is a responsibility.

You need to ask a few questions before you even think about getting a puppy (or if you already have one). A proper understanding of these questions can be very helpful during your puppy-raising journey.

Where Do You Live?

In some apartment buildings, dogs aren't allowed; certain breeds are prohibited in other communities, or weight limits are imposed. You should check with your landlord or homeowners' association to make sure you're following the rules.

Make sure your dog's exercise needs are met by considering your environment. For example, suppose you live in a small apartment in a city. In that case, you may want to consider getting a large, energetic dog that requires lots of exercise and lots of yard space.

You can make an exception (a determined brand-new pet parent will do it), but it's helpful to think this through ahead of time.

Do you have kids?

You can teach your kids how to care for another being and provide them with a loyal, loving friend by having a dog in your home. However, make sure you take your child's age, personality, and the dog's size, age, and temperament into account. Hurting someone isn't a smart idea either. Just remember that a dog is your responsibility, not your kid's.

Do you have any other pets?

Most dogs get along well with other pets in the house -- even cats. Later in this book, we'll introduce a new pet to an existing one. Think about how your current pet will handle the new pet if you have one.

Is this the right time?

Consider whether you can truly take care of a dog right now. Ponder if you're starting a new job, going through a divorce, moving, having a baby, or transitioning through any major life change. Perhaps the best time is when life is less hectic.

Does anyone in your family have a dog allergy?

Try a visit to a friend's house with a dog you're considering to determine whether you'll be allergic to it. Just because someone in your family is allergic doesn't mean you have to give up pet ownership.

What's encouraging you to get a dog?

Would you like a watchdog, a surrogate baby, or a best friend for your child or dog? Do you seek a pet that follows you around all day and cuddles next to you at night, or would you rather one that keeps to himself? Do you plan on taking your pup on six-mile runs every day, or are you just intending to let him out for a few quick walks? Knowing this ahead of time helps you pick the right dog.

Can you accommodate a pet in your home?

If your kid wants a puppy for Christmas, but you're not in the mood for a dog, then you shouldn't go for it. Making the final decision should be left up to the person who will be spending the most time with the dog.

What's your plan for the future?

The average dog lives 10 years or even longer, so think about the future: Are you planning to move? Are you getting married? Planning to have kids? Considering going to grad school? Though we can't always predict the future, it makes sense to contemplate whether a dog will fit into your family for a long time.

Give Your Pup Time

Dogs are highly intelligent, social creatures that need daily mental and physical stimulation. Exercise is critical for an energetic dog, including long runs or extended fetch sessions. Getting the results you want means not cutting corners when it comes to caring for a new dog and training him. Don't get a dog if you work 80 hours a week and cannot take care of it. If you don't have anyone to care for your pet, consider hiring a dog walker.

Additionally, suppose you enjoy being out and about all weekend and don't want to have to go home throughout the day to walk a dog. In that case, you might want to reconsider getting one. Prepare for at least 20 minutes of exercise a day for the first six months to a year. The basics don't take that long to teach; you can accomplish that in under two months. However, you can expect spectacular results if you devote that extra time to training. Because your dogs can live a long time with you, why not invest a little extra time up front to ensure they're well-behaved for years to come?

First, set your expectations clearly. Your new dog will make mistakes and do things you won't like. A potty accident in the house is almost inevitable, and he or she often play bites for months at a time. Your pup will certainly not pick up the toys they leave around the house since they can be noisy and messy. You have to think of getting a dog as normal and remember there is a light at the end of the tunnel. Commit to being patient right now. Dog training involves the paradox that the faster results are sought, the slower you will progress. Slow and steady wins the race.

Raising a Puppy Isn't a Walk-Over

There are tons of problems that are attached to raising a puppy. Biting, potty accidents, jumping, barking, digging... the list goes on!

This isn't to discourage you. No, no!

This is to help you prepare your mind and let you know that it won't be a walk-over. I've gone into thorough details in this book to prepare you for this journey.

Now, the question is: **Are you ready for this?**

CHAPTER 2

A Guide to Choosing the Right Dog

Now that you've decided to be patient - take it slow and steady - I'll walk you through the next most significant thing to consider: choosing a dog.

HOW TO CHOOSE A DOG

If you're ready to get a dog and can take care of one, you should narrow down your choices. Indeed, some people know exactly what kind of dog they want and where to find him, but others have no idea. Whatever you choose, I'll overview the main points.

Puppy or Adult Dog?

People want puppies for obvious reasons- they're the cutest creatures on earth, and there are advantages to getting your dog when he's young. You can start teaching your pet from day one. It's good news that you can prevent bad habits from forming, and you can take steps to avoid socialization issues later on for your dog.

Caring for another living being from an early age is also pretty magical. Keep in mind, though, that puppies are lots of work, and they require a lot of time. Puppies don't know anything about human culture or expectations. They don't come housetrained, and they need to be walked a lot.

They haven't yet figured out that they shouldn't bite. Plus, you have to watch every move they make - puppies are curious and like to chew everything they see, so if you let your guard down, they could wreck your place. Simply put, you'll need extra patience and tolerance.

Are there any advantages to adopting an adult dog?

Well, adult dogs don't play bite as much, and housetraining is less difficult because they have a more developed bladder and can "hold it" longer. Older dogs are typically less expensive to acquire, too. Plus, they're more likely to be fully housetrained, know basic commands such as "sit" and "stay," as well as being fully housebroken. In addition, some of the best dogs in the world came from rescue shelters, where they've waited for years before finding their perfect home.

Nevertheless, some disadvantages may exist...

Some older dogs may not have been socialized correctly as puppies, leading to their lack of confidence in certain situations. Dogs, for instance, fear men simply because they didn't come in contact with them at a young age. It may take longer to break bad habits like destructive chewing, jumping on people, and pulling on a leash if they're already established. If you consider getting a young puppy instead of an older dog, weigh the pros and cons. Remember not to underestimate the commitment a puppy requires. Regardless of age, both a puppy and a mature dog can be a wonderful addition to your family if you have the time and patience to devote to it.

How important is the size?

People may prefer small dogs to carry in their purse; others may believe that bigger dogs are better. Having worked with dogs of all shapes and sizes, I've learned that size has absolutely no bearing on a dog's personality. Nevertheless, it's a key factor to consider.

Take note of these:

There may be a need for more space for exercising large dogs. Generally, this is true.

* ❧ The lifespan of smaller dogs is longer. Chihuahuas can live for 18 years, while Bernese Mountain Dogs only live for six to nine years. Studies published in the *American Naturalist* found that every 4.4 pounds of weight gained decreased life expectancy by one month. The size of a dog will affect its life expectancy and many other factors.
* ❧ A larger dog will cost more to care for in the long run. A large breed will consume 10 times the kibble per day compared with a small breed. Additionally, grooming and toys are more expensive for large dogs.
* ❧ Furthermore, smaller dogs are easier to handle. Picking them up and taking them on errands is much easier. Furthermore, most commercial airlines allow small dogs to be carried on board as carry-ons, provided they

fit in a travel bag under the seat in front of you.

- 🐾 Larger dogs are also effective at scaring strangers away. The appearance of a Bullmastiff in your front window is more likely to scare burglars off than the appearance of a Maltese. However, an attentive, barking small dog can also be an excellent watchdog.
- 🐾 It's easier to control a small dog. It's not that training a small dog is easier. If, however, an 80 pound dog has the same behavioral issues as a 10 pound dog, it's quite different from what it would be like if a 10 pound dog lunged or jumped. Ask yourself if you have the strength to handle a larger dog.

Mixed Breed or Purebred?

While many people focus on one particular breed, I can honestly say that many of the friendliest, most intelligent, and most capable dogs I've ever worked with were mixed breeds. Usually found in shelters, these dogs result from accidental or random breeding. Compared to purebred dogs, they cost much less.

In contrast, it's easy to see why people want a specific breed. They might love Pugs. After all, they grew up with them or German Shepherds because they provide them with a sense of security. Additionally, you can accurately predict your dog's future size, grooming requirements, and appearance with a purebred. You can take a guess when it comes to a mixed breed puppy. Still, you might be surprised when the dog you thought was non-shedding and was going to top out at 10pounds ends up leaving hair all over the house and weighing so much you can't lift him.

Mixing two different breeds leads to what's known as hybrid vigor. By combining two different breeds, you pool from a wider range of traits, so the dog is less likely to have one of the genetic conditions common in certain breeds. An extensive study published by *The Journal of the American Veterinary Medical Association* found that the prevalence of genetic disorders is greatly affected by the health condition of the individual dog.

Until we can determine which one is healthier, we need to conduct more research on the subject. You can rest assured that you'll find a loving, well-behaved companion with so many options.

CHOOSING A BREED

When you choose a purebred dog over a mutt, you need to select a breed. The dangers of focusing too much on breed are too great to be overstated. People often opt for breeds for their dogs based on stereotypes, only to be disappointed when the dog doesn't behave as expected. However, almost no dog meets all of the characteristics defined by a breed description.

I can assure you that you cannot accurately determine the attributes of your dog based on his breed. Many retrievers don't retrieve. These include tiny Yorkies adept at competitive Frisbee, hyper Basset Hounds, and Border Collies terrified of the sheep they were bred to herd. This isn't to say breeds should be ignored altogether. Nevertheless, some breed characteristics remain true, such as shedding and size, which don't vary greatly, so generalizations about them are more accurate.

Furthermore, if you're choosing a dog, try to get a wider perspective on the breed and what it was bred to do - if you want a dog to, say, herd cattle, you may want to stick with a herding breed. Summarily, using breed stereotypes is fine as a starting point for the decision-making process, but only if you understand that these are only guidelines rather than absolutes. Regardless of an owner's race, religion, or culture, every dog also must be assessed individually, just as every human is diverse.

Breed Overview

There are 189 dog breeds recognized by the American Kennel Club (AKC). These breeds are divided into seven segments based on their bred. It's important to realize, however, that exceptions are always possible. There will be dogs that largely fit their stereotypes and others who won't. As an added note, the AKC doesn't have the final say over what constitutes a breed. The AKC doesn't recognize several breeds. But it doesn't diminish their validity.

The following is a breakdown of the main dog groups:

Sporting Group

Spaniels, retrievers, pointers, and setters are breeds created to help hunters flush and retrieve game from land and water. Often, they require a lot of exercises, as they're very active and alert.

Herding Group

The animals in this group are bred to herd other animals, including livestock. Many dogs in this group are intelligent and can often be trained, including German Shepherds, Border Collies, and Welsh Corgis.

Working Group

Rottweilers, Great Danes, Siberian Huskies, and Portuguese Water Dogs were bred to guard livestock, pull sleds, and rescue people. These dogs tend to be intelligent and strong.

Terrier Group

Dogs bred for vermin hunting, such as West Highland White Terriers, Jack Russells, Airedales, and Miniature Schnauzers, can be aggressive and relentless. They may make engaging pets because of their lively personalities.

Toy Group

These dogs, including the Maltese, Havanese, Shih Tzu, and Chihuahua, are small and bred for companionship. They're also called lapdogs.

Hound Group

Many breeds of hunting dogs in this diverse group include Beagles, Basset Hounds, and Dachshunds. Others may have exceptional speed and stamina or other qualities that make hunting easier.

Non-Sporting Group

All dogs that don't seem to fit into any other group belong here, such as Poodles, Shar-Peis, Bichon Frises, and Bulldogs. Their sizes, appearances, and personalities vary greatly.

WHERE TO GET A PUP?

The next step is to search for your perfect pet after doing your research. Here are some perfect places to start.

Shelters and Rescue Groups

Would you like a puppy? How about a purebred? Maybe both? You should start by searching for shelters or rescue groups regardless of what type of dog you're seeking. These nonprofit organizations specialize in one breed and use foster families to care for dogs until they find permanent homes. If you look around, you'll be amazed at how many dogs there are. Approximately 25 percent of dogs in shelters are purebreds, according to the Humane Society of the United States (HSUS).

Many dogs are pregnant in these areas, and their puppies will also need homes. Pet stores may also send puppies to shelters when their puppies don't sell. Consider purchasing the same dog in a pet store one month earlier for a fraction of the price.

Animal shelters take in dogs for a variety of reasons. These reasons range from being abandoned on the side of the road to being abandoned by their owners due to illness or death in their family. Some relinquish based on to an unexpected allergy or a new landlord who doesn't allow dogs. It's also possible for owners to decide they don't want to deal with certain behavior, such as barking or accidents. This is because they don't want to take the time to train their dogs.

Some shelter or rescue dogs, due to their backgrounds, may have difficulties interacting with people or other animals. Your dog may take a few more days to socialize than usual, but you will get there eventually. Many rescued dogs have no idea what their past was like. However, the staff or volunteers will be able to tell you as much about the dog's personality as possible. This is unless the dog just arrived at the shelter or rescue organization that day. Rescued dogs offer so many benefits to owners.

The first benefit is that you provide a home to an animal that is truly in need and might be saving his life. When you buy a dog from a breeder or pet store, the cost is much less. The dog will generally come vaccinated, microchipped, dewormed, and spayed or neutered, saving you hundreds of dollars or even more. There's also the chance of finding an amazing pet at a shelter or rescue group. I've worked with some of the most adorable dogs at shelters and rescue groups.

You can find shelter or rescue dogs in your area by visiting your local shelter or visiting www.theshelterpetproject.org or www.petfinder.com, excellent websites. Likewise, the American Kennel Club provides a rescue network. Don't give up if you don't find the dog you're looking for right away; new animals enter shelters and rescue groups every day.

Breeders

When you're looking for a puppy of a specific breed, a breeder may be the right fit. Some breeders are indeed very knowledgeable about dog breeding. They have extremely high standards and know-how to breed for health and temperament. Their dogs are their pets, and they love them. Still, be careful - there are a lot of unethical breeders out there.

Some people breed dogs strictly for money, and they don't care about the puppies' health or the dogs' welfare. Some people mate their dogs for a little extra money, while others do it as a hobby. Despite their sincere intentions, they don't know much about breeding healthy puppies. How do you find a reputable breeder in a sea of thousands? First of all, ask people you trust for names of recommended breeders —it could be a friend who knows a lot about dogs or your local vet.

It helps if you don't buy a dog from the internet or classified ads since those puppies are usually from puppy mills. Ensure that you see the puppies in person when you're looking for a breeder.

Another sign of a competent breeder is:

- ❧ Takes you to see the puppy's house and lets you meet the mother and, if possible, the father.
- ❧ Sometimes doesn't have puppies for sale.
- ❧ Provides you with a puppy's vaccination schedule, information on the breed, and proof that they screened the parents for breed-related health issues like hereditable cataracts and orthopedic issues. Veterinary records can also prove that the animal has been examined and treated.
- ❧ They ask you a bunch of questions. These breeders won't sell just anyone their puppies.
- ❧ They won't let you take home puppies under eight weeks old.
- ❧ Offers plenty of space for the dogs to run, a clean environment, fresh food and water, and lots of love.
- ❧ If you need references, they're happy to provide them.

Pet Stores

Pet stores sell a lot of dogs that have come from puppy mills. Stopping commercialized breeding is easier if you don't get your dog from a pet store.

Notable exceptions to this rule are stores that offer dogs for adoption in conjunction with shelters, rescue organizations, or other animal control facilities. Some mill dogs don't get enough food, water, socialization, or veterinary care. They sometimes don't even have access to fresh air or sunlight. It's difficult for them to play or exercise, and they lose paws or limbs that get stuck or get infected.

There are cases where dogs are left outside in the elements without any protection. The females are bred as much as possible without a break; and when they're done having a litter, they're sometimes killed. Additionally, the puppy millers may kill the males after breeding them. Puppy mills don't socialize or care for their puppies properly when they're born. These dogs have many health problems due to the poor breeding conditions, resulting in high vet bills for new owners.

Studies have shown that puppies purchased from pet stores are more likely to be aggressive, fearful, and suffer from separation anxiety issues and have difficulties housebreaking than puppies purchased from noncommercial sources. There's a growing backlash against puppy mills. Over 70 different communities in the United States have passed laws outlawing the sale of puppies in pet stores.

In addition, HSUS' Puppy-Friendly Pet Stores Initiative asks pet stores to stop selling puppies raised in commercial breeding facilities and instead adopt pets from local shelters or sell only supplies. The pledge has been signed by about 2,300 pet stores so far. A pet store doesn't mean that you can't find a cute dog, but the odds are stacked against you. If millions of great puppies and adult dogs enter shelters each year, why support puppy mills?

You gave that dog a better life by getting him out of a cage (or crib!) and into your home if you've already bought a dog from a pet store. However, for the reasons I just explained, you should only adopt another dog from a rescue group, shelter, or responsible breeder if you ever decide to get another dog.

CHAPTER 3

Preparing for Your Puppy's Arrival

Your success in training a dog is also dependent on how well you prepare before it finally arrives. It's also best to put so many things in place physically and mentally before bringing a pup in.

But first...

How much money do I need to keep a puppy?

Dog owners often underestimate how much it costs to take care of them. An initial cost can range from a minimal donation at a shelter to $2,000 or more for a pet store or breeder puppy.

You'll have to pay more based on your dog's size and age, its grooming needs, where you live, and your personal preferences. The first thing you need is basic supplies, like a collar, leash, crate, food, a vet checkup, and maybe neutering or spaying. Every year you'll have to spend money on food, vet visits, medications, toys, and supplies. Dog walkers and groomers can also put a big dent in your wallet, as well as dog sitters and trainers when you travel.

Finally, there are those unexpected expenses, like when your dog eats your shoes. If you buy a dog or get one for free from a friend, you'll have to spend anywhere from $1,000 a year to t10 times that.

What equipment is needed for a puppy?

It's vital to get all the necessary items in place to help your dog settle in pretty neatly. By assembling all of your dog's gear before he arrives, you'll provide a stable environment for the pup. The following items should be considered:

Food

Dog Food

Begin by giving the pup familiar foods. Corn-free and grain-free options are great for the start.

Biscuits / Dog Treats

A diet free of sugar, corn syrup, and cane syrup

Edible Bones

It's unsafe to give real bones to dogs since sharp edges can get caught in their mouths or throats. Dogs can chew on edible bones for long periods.

Rawhides

Dogs are less likely to chew your shoes and furniture if you have rawhide chews available. It's important to know that some dogs will swallow quite large chunks of rawhide, causing them to suffer intestinal obstructions.

Fresh Water

If your dog is outside, you can give it fresh water by attaching guzzler attachments to your water spigot.

Water and food bowls

The antibacterial properties of stainless steel bowls prevent bacteria from growing. This will, in turn, keep your dog safe.

Collars & Leashes

Collar

It's safest to have a flat, buckle collar. The breakaway collar reduces the risk of accidental strangulation. If your dog is wearing a slip collar or chain collar, don't leave it unattended. It's not uncommon for dogs to catch their collars when jumping on chain-link fences.

Leash

If your dog pulls, it's a lot easier if you hold a braided leather leash or one with some girth in place of a flat, nylon leash.

Harness or Head Halter

Using a harness or head halter is better than a collar if your dog pulls or has a sensitive neck.

Car Seatbelt or Confinement

If you have a dog in a car, ensure it's restrained with a seatbelt, a gate, or inside a dog crate. Unconstrained dogs aren't permitted to ride in the back of pickup trucks.

Identification tags

Each of your dog's collars should have a permanent tag riveted on it.

Microchip (Optional)

In between your dog's shoulders, your vet can implant an identifying microchip the size of a grain of rice. The chips are scanned by vets and shelters when they receive a new animal.

License for dogs

Every dog must have a county license. Dogs must have rabies vaccinations before they can be licensed.

Muzzle

Basket muzzles are useful in aggressive and emergencies; in pain, a dog may bite if anyone tries to touch him or her.

Cone / Elizabethan Collar

Dogs with cones on their necks are prevented from licking wounds.

Grooming Tools

Dog Shampoo
Dogs shouldn't be washed with human shampoo.

Nail Trimmers
You can either use a dog trimmer or a Dremel.

Ear Cleaning Solutions
It's common to get an ear infection. Ear wax can be reduced by routine flushing.

Brush
For short hair, employ a rubber brush; for long hair, a bristle brush

Dog Toothbrush and Toothpaste
Dogs of small breeds can lose their teeth if they aren't brushed. Soft rubber gloves are ideal for brushing. Peanut butter and liver are common flavors for dog toothpaste.

Chemical Deodorizer for Potty Accidents
It's more likely that dogs will urinate in an area that smells like urine.

Supplies for First Aid
Medicines for diarrhea, Neosporin, Benadryl, antiseptics, etc.

Pickup Bags
You can choose from biodegradable options.

Garbage Can
An item for collecting dog poop and a shovel

Beds & Crates

Dog Crate

A large enough space to allow your dog to turn around and stand up

Beds in Several Rooms

You can provide your dog with a comfortable place to sleep with soft, clean dog beds.

Ex-Pen / Playpen

With these portable pens, your dog can be contained temporarily while still having more room than in a crate.

Training Tools

Bitter Apple Spray

Avoid your dog chewing on objects by spraying on them.

Pedestal

The platform becomes a home for your dog when it's raised.

Toys

There are chew toys, food dispensing toys, rip-apart toys, and tug toys.

How to prepare your living space

As pet parents, your primary responsibility is to keep your dog safe, secure, and comfortable. Give yourself some time before your dog arrives to address each of these responsibilities.

Secure the Perimeter

Upon surveying your dog's new environment, the priority will be to secure the perimeter, both to keep your dog from escaping and keeping people and animals out. A fence should be at least two meters (six feet) high for large dogs, though some can climb higher. Dogs are inventive and will sometimes use an object as a step to get over a fence. It's quite common to see dogs digging under fences. If the first fence is accidentally opened, your dog cannot slip through, so a double fence is helpful in your entrance.

Safety is Key!

Monitor for anything that could harm your dog in the environment. These include poisonous substances and foods such as broken dog bones, loose nails, electrical cables, sharp sticks, or raptors that will attack small dogs, coyotes, or raccoons. To avoid drowning, make sure your dog doesn't swim in a pool that has vertical sides that dogs can't climb out. There's a possibility that a dog may enter a crawl space under the house and become trapped or encounter a snake. Dogs are at risk from temperature hazards as well. You should provide shade and fresh water for your dog during the summer, while he or she will need a warm, heated dog house in the winter. Your dog must sleep inside at night, both for its safety and comfort.

Maintain good hygiene

Having established a secure and safe environment for your dog, we move on to cleaning. By sharing water bowls and feces in common poop areas, dogs can transmit diseases to each other. Daily cleaning and disinfection of kennel floors are necessary for a multi-dog environment. It's also necessary to disinfect water bowls every day to kill bacteria and algae. You should keep food for dogs in an airtight container to prevent bugs and ants from getting into it. Wash your dog's bedding and toys regularly in the washing machine or dishwasher. Ensure that trash and pet waste are removed daily.

Prioritize Dog Comfort

We now turn our attention to the dog's comfort, health, and safety. Dogs should have enough space to run around and soft bedding. Your dog will benefit from having a dedicated potty area with dirt or grass. If there's ice on the ground, your dog may appreciate a coat and booties in winter.

How to Prepare Your Mindset

Having a dog can be frustrating. There are many ways dogs can manipulate situations and take advantage of situations. If you want to avoid flying by the seat of your pants, be prepared with a calm, confident attitude by reviewing the following tips:

Fairness is essential.

Ensure your dog is treated fairly by having clear, specific, and attainable rules, along with consequences that are fair and predictable.

Maintain Consistency

Don't go back on your decisions; be clear about what you want and ask for it consistently.

Motivate with Positive Reinforcement

Reward a dog's good behavior to boost its motivation to please. Rather than focusing on problems, find solutions. Create positive patterns of behavior and success for the dog.

Attention is the Best Reward.

Consider your attention to your dog as the powerful reward that it is. You can give it as a reward for your dog's good behavior and withdraw it as a punishment for his inappropriate behavior.

Instill discipline

Disciplinary action isn't punishment nor hurtful; it's the compassionate application of fair rules. You and your dog can understand the expectations and consequences of discipline if the structure is clear and consistent.

Always Forgive

Deal with misbehavior and let it go, rather than holding a grudge. Be patient and let your dog make amends.

It's also beneficial to include these as well. Identify who will be responsible for the new dog or puppy within your family before he arrives. In addition to being taken out for walks, fed, and played with, the dog also needs to be loved and embraced by the family.

GET YOUR DOG A SUPPORT TEAM

Eventually, you'll have to enlist help to support your dog's needs, even if it doesn't have to happen right away. Here are a few essential roles:

Veterinarian

Throughout its life, your dog will need routine vaccinations.

Emergency Animal Hospital

Find out which emergency facilities have a vet on call after hours.

Pet Insurance

Make sure your dog has medical insurance.

Groomer

Keep an eye on your dog while grooming to ensure you know what's happening.

Pet Sitter

If you're on vacation, ask a professional pet sitter come to your house or even stay there.

Boarding Kennel

Examine how the dogs interact with one another and how often they fight.

Dog Training Lessons

Puppies should attend training classes even when they're young and naive.

Trusted Friend

You should designate a contact person in case of an emergency.

PART 2

FINALLY, THE PUPPY IS HOME. YOUR FIRST DAYS TOGETHER.

CHAPTER 4

Day One - Acquaintance

Your new dog is finally here and ready to go home with you! There's a good chance you're elated, but you may also be nervous about how dependent your dog will be on you. Perhaps you wonder, "How will I teach my pup?" How should I feed it? How can I keep my dog from destroying my house? "How can I ensure that I give it the necessary attention with my busy schedule?"

You should think about these things if you aren't already. A new dog can be exciting, but don't forget the responsibilities that come with it.

However, don't worry! No matter if you carefully selected the perfect dog for your family or if you bought a dog on a whim and feel as if you may have bitten off more than you can chew, I'll point you in the right direction from day one.

It won't be easy to adapt to having your dog as a regular part of your life right away. In the same way, it takes some time for a dog to adjust to a new environment. The pup won't know what to do, so you'll have to be patient and have a lot of tolerance. As a result, things won't go exactly as planned. And that's okay! This chapter will prepare you for a smooth transition.

INTRODUCTION TO THE NEW FAMILY

First greetings with family members can be a pleasant or chaotic experience for your dog. With the steps in this chapter, you can teach your dog his name and learn how to interact politely with you and your family members.

Set a harmonious tone for your home from the very beginning. Your dog must understand that it may not bully or overrun your child or the cat. Ensure that your dog interacts calmly with other family pets. Educate the children in your home on how to act respectfully toward their dog and how to de-escalate potentially stressful situations.

You should introduce one new variable at a time when allowing your dog to meet your kids or other pets. It isn't a wise idea to bring all your relatives, friends, and neighbors over right now. Keep it within the immediate family at first to maintain a calm environment. Additionally, you should take it easy; suddenly allowing your dog to interact with your cat, for instance, can be disastrous. Take the time to do this.

The following tips will make your family introduction go smoothly:

Introducing Children

Dogs bite more than 4.5 million people each year, according to the American Veterinary Medical Association. Not only are children the most likely victims, but they're also the most likely to be seriously injured.

For that reason, kids must be taught to respect the space of dogs. Children shouldn't interrupt a dog while eating or sleeping, and they should never rush over to a dog while it's eating or sleeping. Since dealing with kids is more difficult than it appears, you must constantly monitor all interactions between your dog and children. A crucial part of that is making good first impressions with your child.

Control the situation first. You don't want a dog to knock a toddler over, but you don't want a child to pull on a puppy's tail either. Ensure that your child is gentle with the pet. When a child gives the dog a special treat such as chicken, the first meeting usually improves. This tells the dog, at the most basic level, "I'm good, and you can trust me."

From a few feet away, have the child throw a piece of meat at the dog. Whenever your dog is unfamiliar with something, you should use distance to help the pup adjust.

Additionally, if your dog has an unpleasant habit of grabbing treats roughly, tossing the food will make things more peaceful. Make sure the dog is allowed to approach your child. Don't smother them with their new pet. Try to interact with your dog briefly and positively. When the dog has finished the treat and seems comfortable, ask your child to sit on the ground and gently pet it.

Despite how excited he or she may be about her new family member, your child is responsible for the dog. You shouldn't discourage your kids from playing with and caring for the family dog; however, you need to set realistic expectations. When kids are older than 12, they can help train the family pet if they're serious about it, but younger kids are unlikely to be able to train your dog.

Introducing Other Family Dogs

One out of three families with dogs has two or more. Nevertheless, if you are adding a second (or third!) pup to the family, it's important to ensure the introduction goes smoothly. You should usually introduce your dogs in a place neither dog considers its own home if you already have one. Putting both dogs on a leash in your neighborhood or at a park might be a good idea. Just use caution and common sense.

Ensure that both dogs are tired before attempting to control them. Dogs are generally physically satisfied with enough exercise, less likely to react unfavorably and typically easier to control. You can start by separating the dogs and seeing how they react to it. Avoid forcing the introduction of the dogs. Let them meet at their own pace, even if they ignore each other initially. They should then slowly sniff each other and get to know one another. As a precaution, perhaps you should separate them for a few minutes to give them a breather before trying again.

We should ease dogs into new situations as much as possible. Bring both dogs home and repeat these steps outside your home at first if they seem friendly and accepting of each other. Then, take them inside. It's okay to take the leashes off if the dogs still seem to be doing well and there are no red flags such as nipping or one of them attempting to run away or tucking his tail between his legs. Dogs may play fight, and an older dog might growl at the new dog if the younger dog is jumping all over. It's quite normal to some extent.

You should break up rough play between your dogs if you feel they are playing too rough. Children often play rough with their siblings. It may start with them playing and getting along, but things can quickly escalate into a squabble. Although they may need time apart from each other to cool down, they can still play together. However, you should limit their access to one another as much as possible if you notice there's consistently a lot of growling, serious altercations are regularly occurring, or one or both dogs seem particularly aggressive towards one another.

Introducing the Family Cat

It's common for cats and dogs to be portrayed as mortal enemies. But I've seen plenty of dogs get along with their feline companions. Some even become best buds. You just have to tread lightly when introducing your cat to the new dog to avoid any problems. You should make sure your dog has gotten enough exercise before he meets your cat for the first time. Dogs with pent-up energy are less likely to behave well in new situations.

When you have a puppy, it's usually easier to introduce him to a cat because, let's be honest, cats are pretty good at outsmarting puppies.

Before you introduce your puppy to your cat, make sure its claws are trimmed. Start by keeping the puppy on a leash, so he doesn't suddenly run toward the cat and get injured. As an alternative, you can put the puppy in a crate that your cat is okay with and let her sniff around. It's vital to gradually let the two animals get used to each other, which can take a few days to weeks. Treats are a good way to help your dog become comfortable with cats. Plus, if you give them treats, dogs tend to focus more on you during the introduction. You have to concentrate more on the cat if you have an older, larger dog, especially one with lots of energy.

Keep them separated at first, then introduce them under very controlled circumstances for days to weeks, maybe even months. If you choose a dog with no history of aggression towards other animals, you'll get off to a great start. Keep the dog on a leash or put the cat in a crate. Keep the introductions brief and controlled. Then you can briefly let the dog off-leash to see how they'll interact once you see the dog isn't lunging toward the cat and barking, and the cat isn't hissing and in a crouched stance with her ears back.

Whenever you see anything in their body language that makes you uneasy, intervene and take your time to get to know them. A dog shouldn't be introduced to the family cat too soon. Usually, that doesn't work.

No matter how old your dog is, make sure your cat has a safe place by using a cat door, baby gate, or even a window sill that only the cat can access. Make sure she can get to her food, water, and litter box. Be sure the animals can't directly interact with each other when you're not around. This shouldn't be a problem if you're using a dog crate, gates, or dog-proofed areas.

Introducing the Leash

After your dog is home for a few days, you should introduce the pup to the leash.

If you have an older dog, he's probably used to wearing a leash; however, if you have a puppy or dog that's not used to them, he or she might panic if they feel any tension on them. Put yourself in the dog's shoes. This must be pretty freaky since the animal has never been restrained before. This is why we want to be proactive about encouraging our dogs to take to this new gadget.

I'll show you how:

1. Start by letting your dog sniff and explore the leash for a minute. You can hold it or put it on the ground. It's to reiterate that there's something new in the room to learn about. When you're in this phase, introduce treats to make the leash more positive. When the leash comes out, we want to let the pup know that awesome stuff comes with it.

2. In your living room or familiar environment, hook the leash to your dog's harness or collar and let it go for a walk. Don't let any tension build upon the leash at first. Let's change the variables little by little. The leash may seem like a toy at first, so your dog will grab it and run around. Although we'll correct this behavior down the road, it's more important that the dog is happy for now.

3. Once your dog has walked around for a while with the leash behind him, use a high-pitched voice or a fun sound to get the pup to come to you. Offer a tasty treat for increased cooperation. Pick up the leash very gently for one second, making sure not to put any tension on it. Let your dog have a treat as if to say, "I like the way you reacted to that first test." See what we did there? By starting very small, we greatly increased the chances of favorable behavior. You'll use the same theme in almost every instance of teaching your dog. Taking this first step might seem silly, but your dog will learn much more quickly if you break things down into smaller steps.

4. Whenever you introduce a revolutionary concept, it's always wise to reward generously as you're holding the leash for long periods. If your dog starts bucking or panicking, don't be discouraged. It's just a signal to slow down.

5. Last but not least, practice holding the leash with one hand. Walk around the house and entice your dog with treats while holding one in your hand. If your dog has a burst of energy that results in tension on the leash, and it doesn't panic, reward the pup immediately with an extra treat. Whenever it panics, you can release the leash and ask the dog to come to you. Most dogs just need a period to adjust to being on a leash; it's okay if it takes a few days for them.

Introducing the Crate

Crates are one of the best tools you can use to train your dog. If you aren't around to watch your dog, the crate keeps it safe. Additionally, it can be helpful in housetraining your dog and preventing destructive behaviors such as chewing up your belongings.

This is why you should introduce your dog to his crate as soon as possible. Many people seem to think crates are cruel, like imprisoning a dog. Dogs can be irritable in crates if they spend too much time in them or if the crates are too small. Have you ever noticed how some dogs prefer to sleep under couches or tables, or love to burrow into closets or other dark places?

It's no secret that dogs prefer quiet, cozy nooks, and crates are no exception. You can make the crate a comfortable place for your pet if you introduce it in a fun way and use it properly. So, where do you begin? In my experience, putting your dog in a crate and shutting the door will only scare it and set you back.

People typically make two common crate mistakes - putting the dog in the crate too quickly and closing the door before the dog is ready. Here's a better way:

🐾 Let your dog follow you into the crate by throwing it a tasty treat. Allow him to leave, so he sees that there's an exit available. Keep doing it over and over.

🐾 After that, repeat the exercise, but this time close the door for a few seconds. You should then immediately let your dog out, reward it with a treat, and say, "Yes, great dog!"

🐾 As you increase your dog's time inside his crate, keep the door closed for a few days. Find out below whether or not you should crate your puppy on its first night at home. It's best to take your time when doing this.

🐾 Once your dog has spent time in the crate while you're present, try stepping out of the room and observe how your dog reacts when you aren't there. Initially, you should ignore mild whining; however, if your dog shows more extreme crying or distress, let the pup out and take a break from crate training. If necessary, repeat the process.

🐾 Getting an older dog accustomed to crates shouldn't be a problem if it already has a positive association with them. Nevertheless, some dogs will absolutely hate their crates, especially if they previously had negative experiences with them. They tend to do this, especially if they've been left in them too long, which is common with puppies from puppy mills and neglectful pet owners. If that's the case, consider a puppy-proofed laundry room or bathroom or a playpen.

FEEDING

There are almost as many dog food options as human food options, making determining what is healthy and what isn't very easy. You can get caught up in marketing tactics, and if you ask others for their opinion, you'll get a variety of answers. Personal taste is usually the deciding factor.

Consider these factors, however:

How Should I Choose a Dog Food?

Whenever I choose dog food, I carefully read the ingredient list, considering that quantities are listed first. Avoiding brands that contain cheap ingredients, such as corn, and those with questionable ingredients is always a good idea. As a substitute, I prefer a quality protein such as chicken or fish as the first ingredient.

If you choose a food, make sure it states that it meets the nutritional requirements for your pet based on its life stage, as stated by the Association of American Feed Control Officials - AAFCO.

Additionally, it must include a guaranteed analysis that lists the nutrient percentages, and it must meet certain requirements, like a minimum percentage of crude protein and crude fat and a maximum percentage of crude fiber and moisture.

It's important not to be misled by sneaky marketing ploys. For instance, just like with human food, many terms like "whole food" or "natural" are unregulated, so they don't hold much weight when you see them in a bag. Instead, you should consult your veterinarian to determine the best food for your dog based on its age, size, activity level, and any health needs.

Some people work at pet supply stores who are very knowledgeable and might be able to assist you. You can also find reviews of many brands at www.dogfoodadvisor.com. Depending on your dog's needs, your vet can recommend either dry food or wet food, or even a combination of the two. In the event that you plan to make your dog's food yourself, you may want to consult your veterinarian. The decision is also up to your dog, so you may have to try a couple of options.

How Often Should Your Dog Be Fed?

It's recommended that puppies eat two to three meals a day up until they are around six months old. After that, you can give your dog food once or twice a day, depending on its age, size, and eating and exercising habits. Free-feeding is a practice where dogs are fed at the beginning of each day and allowed to graze all day.

When housetraining, I've found that keeping a schedule is the best method, as you can more easily predict when your dog needs to go out. Schedules are also the best way to ensure that every dog eats his or her own food in households with multiple dogs.

How much food does your dog need?

Feeding your dog depends a lot on your dog's age, size, metabolism, and exercise habits, as well as general recommendations on the bag. Check the recommendations on the bag to get an idea of how much your dog should eat. Agility dog competitors need more calories than a couch potato of the same breed, age, and size.

Consult your veterinarian for the ideal amount for your dog, and then watch your pet to ensure that it maintains a healthy weight. If you want to feel its ribs but not see them, then you should be able to do so. If your dog is getting too bulky, you can help the pup lose weight by limiting his or her treats, cutting back on portions, and increasing exercise, all under the guidance of a veterinarian, of course!

Food Allergies to Consider

Allergies to various foods can occur in dogs, including beef, dairy products, chicken, lamb, fish, eggs, corn, wheat, and soy. These allergies vary from one dog to another. An allergic dog may also be allergic to other ingredients if it's allergic to one. Additionally, it may eat a certain food for months or even years and then suddenly develop an allergy to it.

Itchy skin and ear inflammation, vomiting and diarrhea are some of the symptoms of a food allergy in dogs. You can treat your dog if it appears to be allergic to a certain food. Ask your veterinarian for more information. To determine the exact cause, the professional may prescribe a hypoallergenic diet or a portion of special food.

Raw food diets

Dog food comes in many varieties. BARF diets, for example, are either known as Bones and Raw Food or Biologically Appropriate Raw Food. In theory, dogs should eat raw meat, bones, and organs as their ancestors did in the wild. There are claims that this type of diet offers health benefits like shinier coats, cleaner teeth, healthier skin, and more energy, though no studies have been conducted to support those claims.

Many veterinary doctors, the American Veterinary Medical Association, the Centers for Disease Control and Prevention, and countless other organizations warn of the dangers of a raw food diet for pets, including E-coli and other food-borne diseases, as well as bones puncturing the organs.

Furthermore, a study in the *Journal of the American Veterinary Medical Association* looked at raw food diets and found that some may cause dogs' health problems. It's totally your choice what your dog eats, of course. As a result, I highly recommend that you work closely with your veterinarian to provide your dog with a balanced diet. Nevertheless, I advocate avoiding a BARF diet because the risks outweigh the potential benefits.

THE FIRST NIGHT

A magical first day can quickly turn into a nightmare when it is time for bed. It's not as pleasant when the cute little pup wakes you up at 3 in the morning. Sure, it's adorable, but you should get some sleep!

Keep your expectations realistic here, and don't expect a good night's sleep right away, even if your dog sleeps through the night. Owning a puppy may require you to wake up occasionally during the first few weeks.

You and your dog will both sleep well as your dog gets adjusted. The process of getting your dog on a schedule can take a few weeks, so be patient. When a puppy is about 12 weeks old, most will sleep through the night for about eight hours.

During the first night, your dog may be scared, lonely, and confused. A puppy may be leaving his mother and littermates for the first time. It's usually best to let your dog sleep in your room for the first few nights, regardless of whether you intend to let it stay there permanently. Your pup will need some comfort during this time. It's ideal to keep a dog crate next to your bed. You should get your dog used to the crate during the day, whether or not it seems extra wary of it at first. The pup probably won't be too happy in it at night if he or she isn't used to it during the day.

If you want to secure his leash to your bed or nightstand, you can put some old towels or blankets down next to your bed. Don't let it chew anything, and don't let it get tangled. What matters is that your pet gets age-appropriate exercise during the day, so that it's less stressed and more likely to sleep at night. Try ignoring your dog at first if it cries or whines at night. It isn't a good idea to pick the pup up right away-that could teach that whining gets an instant response of "get out of the crate and play."

It's okay to take your dog out if it has been crying for 20 minutes or longer and you've already walked it. It's fine if you don't do it all the time, just on the first few days while the pup is getting used to it. Many people lose patience when it comes to bedtime but don't. In this respect, getting a new dog is like getting a new baby. You should be sympathetic to what your puppy just went through.

Ensure that your pup feels safe and comfortable. You and your dog will sleep through the night in no time.

CHAPTER 5

How to Monitor a Puppy's Health?

Pup parents are responsible for making sure their pets are safe. And what that means is that you need to be well aware of all that affects your puppy's health. Thus, all that you need to know about pup health will be discussed in this chapter.

UNDERSTANDING PUPPY HEALTH

There are tons of dog-associated diseases out there and too many to number. Here's how to handle them.

Vaccinations

To prevent serious illnesses, dogs require certain vaccinations, just like humans. An example: Parvovirus is a highly contagious viral illness that causes vomiting, lethargy, severe diarrhea, and dehydration. The infection can even cause death.

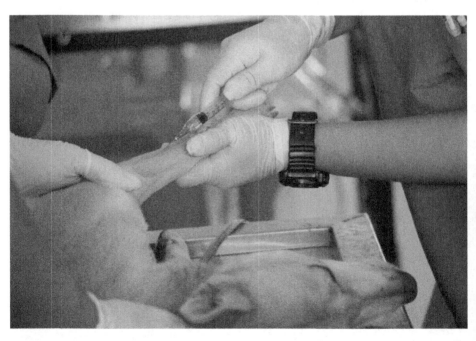

However, it should be noted that vaccines come with some health risks, such as soreness and allergic reactions, so you should discuss your pet's needs with your veterinarian. Vaccinations should begin around six weeks and then be administered every three weeks until the puppy is 16 weeks old (except for rabies, which is given once between 12 and 16 weeks at the very least). Veterinarians recommend revaccinating adult dogs every one to three years, depending on the vaccine, the dog's health, and the environment.

The American Animal Hospital Association updated its dog vaccine guidelines in 2011. Vaccinations are divided into "Core" vaccines, which are universally recommended, and "Noncore" vaccines, which are optional. Talk to your vet to determine which ones your dog needs.

Here are the breakdowns:

CORE

- Canine distemper virus
- Canine adenovirus 2
- Canine parvovirus 2
- Rabies

NONCORE

- Bordetella
- Leptospirosis

- Lyme disease
- Canine parainfluenza virus
- Canine influenza
- Measles (puppies younger than six weeks or breeding females)

Parasites

Dogs are susceptible to different parasites throughout their lives, from fleas and ticks to worms and Giardia. Let's take a look.

External Parasites: Fleas and Ticks

In addition to being a notorious enemy of all dogs, fleas cause serious problems for both animals and humans alike. Fleas are notorious for spreading the plague! The flea is a wingless insect that jumps from host to host, eating a pup's blood. Anemia is one of the problems they may cause for dogs, as is tapeworm, when a flea carrying tapeworm eggs is ingested and it then triggers allergies.

Immediately contact your veterinarian if your dog exhibits any flea symptoms, including excessive licking or scratching, hair loss, hot spots, and flea dirt, which appears as dirt but is actually flea droppings. An effective flea treatment may include a special shampoo or liquid that kills the fleas and their eggs. If the infestation is severe, call a local exterminator to see how they can eliminate the fleas from your yard; these professionals can also suggest other ways to eradicate the fleas from your home.

For example, the first steps might include washing all bedding in hot water, vacuuming all carpets, and then disposing of the vacuum bags. The tick, on the other hand, is an arachnid. As with fleas, they can sap blood from their hosts, resulting in anemia. They can also transmit dangerous illnesses, including Lyme disease, Rocky Mountain spotted fever and Ehrlichia.

You can remove ticks from dogs by putting on a pair of disposable gloves, rubbing alcohol, and tweezers. Ensure that the tick is pulled straight out (don't twist it!) and that no part of the critter is left behind. Your veterinarian can identify which type of tick is responsible for your dog's illness if the tick is preserved in a closed container with rubbing alcohol. You should thoroughly wash the tick site on your dog and call your vet to discuss further treatment options. It's best to prevent fleas and ticks each year-there are topical medications and oral pills that prevent both parasites simultaneously. Check for fleas and ticks frequently on your dog's bedding and living area, especially if you live in a humid or woody area.

Internal Parasites: Worms, Giardia, and Coccidia

In addition to contracting external parasites, dogs can also contract internal parasites. These parasites can spread throughout the body, causing a range of health complications. You should work closely with your doctor to prevent or treat these parasites as soon as you notice any symptoms.

Let's break it down:

🐾 Heartworm

Parasitic roundworms can grow up to 12 inches and can live for up to seven years inside the arteries and hearts of animals. Those who have been bitten by mosquitoes have spread the parasite and may suffer from weight loss, coughing, and difficulty breathing, which ultimately can cause heart failure and lead to death.

In spite of heartworms commonly occurring in mosquito-prone areas like the Gulf of Mexico, the Atlantic Ocean, and along the Mississippi River, they are reported in all fifty states. Concerning heartworm disease, the Food and Drug Administration (FDA) has approved two drugs; however, they're both very expensive and toxic to dogs. You should take preventive measures throughout the year.

In addition to topical liquids, oral tablets, and injectables, the FDA has approved several products to prevent heartworm disease. Discuss what type is right for your dog with your veterinarian.

🐾 Other Worms

Roundworms, tapeworms, hookworms, and whipworms can all infest the dog's intestines, causing serious health complications such as diarrhea, anemia, and severe lethargy. Animals can transmit roundworms and hookworms to humans, which makes them zoonotic.

Consult your veterinarian if your dog experiences diarrhea, changes in her appetite or coat, or excessive coughing. You can also find worms in your dog's stool or under its tail. You should still take further steps to protect your dog despite the deworming that it probably received as a puppy.

For instance, tapeworms are transmitted by fleas, so a flea prevention regimen is essential. You can probably protect your dog against the majority of worms with the medicine you give it for heartworm prevention. Can you protect yourself and the rest of your family? If your dog does have worms, good hygiene, such as washing your hands as needed, will keep you from catching them.

❖ Giardia and Coccidia

They can cause your dog's gastrointestinal lining to be damaged, limiting the nutrients she can absorb from her food. They also trigger diarrhea. These parasites are highly contagious, single-celled, and zoonotic. They can, however, be eliminated by medication, when discovered.

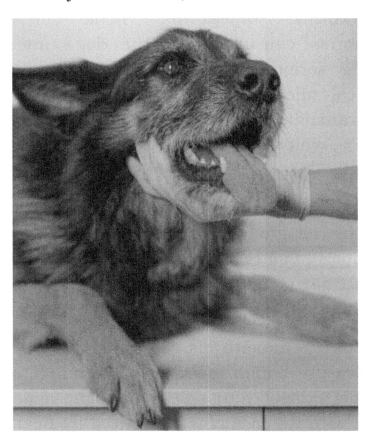

Vomiting

The act of vomiting involves your dog forcefully ejecting the contents of his or her stomach or upper intestine. Symptoms of vomiting include nausea and abdominal heaving.

There are several reasons why dogs vomit. It's possible that your dog ate too much or too quickly, or too much grass. This can sometimes be a more serious problem. There's a possibility that your dog swallowed something toxic, or it could be a sign of a serious illness that requires a vet visit. You should understand the difference between an isolated case of vomiting and chronic vomiting.

You can tell whether your dog is vomiting or regurgitating. A dog typically regurgitates shortly after eating, and it's mostly a passive process - the dog lowers their head, and food comes up without any active abdominal contractions like during vomiting. Regurgitation usually results in undigested food that isn't bile-containing. In contrast, vomit contains some bile but is partially digested. Dogs almost always eat regurgitated food.

What Causes My Dog to Throw Up?

For the best treatment, it's critical to determine the root cause of your dog's vomiting. Among the causes of a sudden or acute episode of vomiting are:

- 🐾 Intestinal parasites
- 🐾 Pancreatitis
- 🐾 Intestinal inflammation
- 🐾 Bacterial infections (gastrointestinal tract)
- 🐾 Intestinal obstruction
- 🐾 Ingestion of toxic substances
- 🐾 Certain medications
- 🐾 Diet change
- 🐾 Kidney failure
- 🐾 Food intolerances
- 🐾 Acute kidney failure
- 🐾 Bloat
- 🐾 Parvovirus
- 🐾 Ingestion of foreign objects (toys, garbage)
- 🐾 Acute liver failure
- 🐾 Viral infections
- 🐾 Heatstroke
- 🐾 Constipation
- 🐾 Cancer
- 🐾 Liver failure
- 🐾 Colitis
- 🐾 Uterine infection
- 🐾

Why is my dog throwing up frequently?

Frequent vomiting could indicate a serious illness. Monitor for these symptoms:

- Pain in the abdomen
- Weakness
- Vomit with blood in it
- Depression
- Weight loss
- Dehydration
- Fever

If your dog is vomiting food and exhibiting any of these symptoms, take it to the vet right away. Your dog throwing up and eating normally might just be an isolated incident. Speak to your veterinarian if your dog vomits and doesn't eat.

FINDING A VET

Getting to know your vet before you bring your dog home is important. The first reason is that you don't want to make a hasty decision because your dog urgently needs medical care.

You should also have your new pet examined by a vet within 48 hours of bringing it home, even if a vet examined it at the place where you found the pup. Because of their immature immune systems and the possibility of catching an illness from one of the many other animals they lived with, dogs, especially those from shelters and puppy stores, often come home with minor illnesses.

If your dog has a cough, for example, you can make sure she gets the antibiotics she needs before it becomes pneumonia. A veterinarian can treat an eye infection before it becomes much worse. Furthermore, a veterinarian can tell you whether your new dog has any potentially life-threatening health issues that might require more time and money than you have available. When problems are discovered early, you can make the difficult decision to return the dog, if necessary.

Those with dogs can ask their friends and family for recommendations for a vet. There are also online review sites such as www.yelp.com or www.angieslist.com. Clinics and hospitals that the American Animal Hospital Association has accredited are likely to provide excellent care-although many wonderful practices aren't accredited. Once you have several options on the table, check out the vets' offices to determine which one is right for your pet.

Here's what to look for:

- The facilities should be clean, and the receptionists, assistants, and other employees should be helpful and friendly.
- How do they treat clients on the phone? Do they treat the animals nicely?
- Determine how many veterinarians work there. If it's a large practice, ask if your dog

will see the same doctor every time. Sometimes having multiple vets on staff is a benefit because they each have a different area of expertise. If it's a smaller practice, ask who will cover for the vet if he's on vacation or out of the office.

* Ask about office hours and how they handle emergencies. Will you have to go to another clinic if, say, your dog needs medical attention at 3 A.M.? Who will monitor your pet if she needs to stay overnight? Will the vet return phone calls directly, and if so, when? What kinds of services does he or she offer, and will he or she refer you to a specialist if need be?

* Find out about the vet's education. The vet should have received a veterinary medical degree from a school accredited by the American Veterinary Medical Association. The professional should also have plenty of experience, particularly with your dog's breed.

* Consider location. How far are you willing to drive for regular checkups? What about emergencies?

* Inquire about which forms of payment the vet practice will accept. Keep in mind that most practices won't accept insurance (that is, they won't bill the insurance company on

your behalf, as most human health care providers will); however, they'll help you fill out the claim so that the insurance company can reimburse you.

- ❧ For questions regarding how to prepare for the arrival of your dog, schedule an appointment with your veterinarian. Does the professional seem knowledgeable? Does he or she communicate clearly? Does he or she take the time to answer your questions? Are you happy with the doctor's demeanor, and do you agree with one's overall philosophies about raising a dog?

- ❧ If you (or your dog) don't click with the vet for any reason at any point, you can always look for another one.

When to Book a Visit

Aside from your annual checkups, schedule an appointment with your vet if you notice any of these symptoms:

- ❧ Vomiting
- ❧ Incontinence or abnormal bowel habits
- ❧ Eating habits change, appetite decreases, or excessive water consumption occurs
- ❧ Eye discharges, nose discharges, or discharge from other body openings
- ❧ An out-of-the-ordinary behavior, such as excessive lethargy or sudden withdrawal
- ❧ aggressiveness
- ❧ Increased salivation
- ❧ Hair loss that's out of the ordinary; dandruff
- ❧ Any part of a dog's body that has a foul breath or odor
- ❧ A lump, a sore, or an open wound
- ❧ An inability to get up or lie down or a limp
- ❧ Excessive licking, biting, or scratching of any part of the body or shaking of the head.

CHAPTER 6

Puppy Care and First Exercise

In the same way as small children, dogs completely rely on us for their health and wellbeing, from grooming to dental care to exercise and diet. Additionally, you'll bond with your pet more deeply if you always protect and care for it!

Help your dog maintain a healthy weight, make sure she gets enough exercise, neuter or spay her, do what you can to keep her parasite-free and take your pup to the vet for regular vaccinations to identify any problems early.

Your veterinarian is your dog's most important health partner. Please use the guidelines I outlined on this page, chapter 5, to help you choose wisely. Kindly consult your veterinarian to determine which health care measures are best for your dog. This chapter will give you an overview of general care, grooming, and dog exercise.

HOW TO GROOM A PUP

Taking care of your dog requires regular grooming; the amount of grooming will vary based on your dog's coat, age, and where you live. Here are some basic guidelines:

Nails

Your dog's nails should be kept short at all times. In addition to scratching you and your furniture, they also snag on carpets or hinder your dog's ability to walk. It can be tricky to cut them properly-cut too deep, and you'll cause your dog a lot of pain and bleeding.

Alternatively, you can ask your groomer or veterinarian to show you how to do it correctly. Teach your dog a good association with having nails trimmed once you know the proper technique. You can, for example, show the pup the nail clipper and let the dog smell it, then put the nail trimmer around its nail, and let it feel how it feels.

Take it slow! After each small step, reward your dog when it behaves calmly, gradually allowing you to cut the nails. It won't take a dog long to become accustomed to having them trimmed!

Teeth

Everyone knows how important it is to brush their teeth. What makes dogs any different? Your dog should have its teeth brushed every day. In addition to keeping breath fresh, it can also prevent periodontal disease (gum disease), which is common among dogs and is associated with serious health issues such as heart, liver, and kidney problems. Pet supply stores sell dog toothbrushes or finger brushes.

You should never use human toothpaste because it contains high-foaming detergents that a dog could swallow or inhale-they don't know how to spit it out! Until you find a flavor your dog enjoys, try a variety of flavors of dog toothpaste. Ensure your dog has plenty of dental treats and soft toys to chew on, as well as quality food. Some products marketed as "dental diets" contain plaque-reducing ingredients.

Depending on your pup's dental and other health needs, your vet can recommend the best food and treats for your dog. According to the American Veterinary Dental College, ask your veterinarian about plaque and tartar preventative measures to prevent periodontal disease. Likewise, contact a professional if you detect any symptoms of dental disease such as loose or discolored teeth, bad breath, drooling, dropping food, or a loss of appetite.

A vet should examine your dog's mouth during the wellness examination, or any vet visit, for that matter.

Eyes

As a means of communicating with your dog, it's essential to look into the dog's eyes regularly. You can use a moist cotton ball to remove any buildup in the corners when you do so. It's vital to keep your dog's hair out of her eyes not to irritate them. Whenever you notice an eye infection like redness, cloudiness, excessive discharge, crusting, squinting, or the third eyelid showing, contact your veterinarian immediately.

In the case of rusty-looking tear stains at the corner of your dog's eyes, which can be especially noticeable on white dogs, see your vet to determine a possible cause such as allergies or problems with its tear ducts. Talk to your veterinarian if the stains bother you, as there are products you can sprinkle on your dog's food to eliminate the stains potentially.

Ears

Cotton balls and cleaning solutions (consult your vet for specific recommendations) are needed to regularly clean your dog's ears. With a new cotton ball, dab the outside of the earflap and then slowly work your way into the ear, stopping whenever you feel resistance. If the cotton balls become very dirty, that could be a sign of an ear infection, so see your veterinarian right away. Infections can also cause swelling, redness, crusting, and an odor in the ear. Likewise, schedule an appointment to ensure all is well if your dog scratches one's ear a lot, rubs it on the floor, or appears to be off-balance. A parasite infection may cause the pup's ear to itch and inflame, implying that it has ear mites.

Coat

For some dogs, brushing every day is necessary to prevent matting and excessive shedding, while others only need brushing every few weeks or even less frequently. Your veterinarian or professional groomer can advise you on the right kind of combs and brushes to use. Those with long hair may require a rubber brush and a slicker brush, while those with a short, smooth coat may need a rubber brush and a bristle brush. Not all dogs love to be brushed. So, go at a slow pace if your pet doesn't.

To begin, let your dog sniff the brush, then gently touch her with it, and gently stroke her with the brush once. Be sure to reward every step. As you brush your dog's coat, look for fleas, flea dirt (little black specks left behind by flea droppings), ticks, lesions or irritated areas on his skin that may need medical attention. Always brush gently!

Bath Time

According to some experts, dogs should be bathed weekly; others suggest bathing them less frequently, such as monthly. It depends on your lifestyle. You'll probably want to ensure that your dog is clean and free from debris if it sleeps in your bed with you. Some people even carry their dogs into the shower with them! You can bathe your dog in a regular bathtub or a small portable plastic tub.

You should avoid getting any water or shampoo in your dog's ears, eyes, or nose; don't just dump water on her head. To ensure your dog's safety, you might want to put cotton balls in his ears. Also, always use mild shampoos designed specifically for dogs; consult your vet or groomer to determine which is best. In addition, if your dog gets a weekly bath, make sure that its skin doesn't become dry or itchy; if this happens, either reduce the baths or use a moisturizing shampoo that will help keep the pup's skin soft.

PHYSICAL EXERCISES

Staying fit and healthy requires regular exercise. This is also true for dogs. They warrant physical activity to stay healthy. Often, we forget to exercise our dogs because life gets so busy.

How Much Exercise Do Dogs Need?

As a general rule, dogs should exercise one to two hours per day to stay healthy. Depending on your dog's age, breed, and tolerance, they may need more or less. Shih Tzus may want to lounge on the couch, while Border Collies, Rhodesian ridgebacks, or Bluetick Coonhounds may perform agility for four hours every day and still want more. Finding your dog's exercise requirements may take some trial and error, as no two dogs are alike. You should give your dog as much exercise as it wants, but take it slow.

If you're starting a new exercise program for your dog, make sure to start slowly and let your dog build up endurance and tolerance to the exercise. Look out for signs of exhaustion; they may include heavy panting, lameness, wheezing, disorientation, and slowing or stopping to lie down during activities. Don't let your dog out on hot days unless it has access to fresh, cool water. Your dog may appear tired, achy, or disinterested in exercise if he or she is tired, achy, or disinterested in exercise. Call your vet if you spot any signs of illness while exercising.

What's the Best Exercise for My Dog?

Exercise and your dog can go hand in hand with several activities. Although some activities provide your dog with more exercise than you, they're still fun. Walk your dog to a dog park, or play fetch with a ball. Have you thought about participating in dog sports with your dog? Competitions in agility, catch, and herding are great places to begin.

Let's start something fun and introduce a new type of exercise to your dog. While keeping your dog healthy, it's a wonderful way to bond.

❧ Taking a walk

We tend to give our dogs walks as the classic form of exercise. It's okay, though. Most dogs love walking!

A walk is a wonderful way for your dog to explore the world with her nose in addition to getting some exercise. Take your time. Your dog can explore as much as he or she likes on the walk. Make sure your dog sees and smells something new now and then by taking a different route.

❧ Running

Some dogs enjoy running as an exercise. Not all dogs can indeed tolerate this type of exercise, but it's a necessity for some!

Using a hands-free leash can make running with your dog easier. Safety and legal considerations make off-leash running unwise. Nevertheless, it might be considered if your dog has a truly reliable recall and local laws allow dog's off-leash.

Start slowly; then kick up your speed and distance when running with your dog. Hot asphalt can burn your paws, so avoid running in high temperatures. Check in regularly with your dog to monitor its exercise tolerance and ensure that it's getting the necessary breaks.   Bring plenty of water along on runs.

❖ Cycling

Some dogs aren't built to run alongside your bike. This can pose a risk to both you and your pet. It can still be fun to ride a bike with your dog if you do it correctly. It would be best if you started slowly. Make sure your dog gets used to the bike. Continue running and keep up with her as she gets used to it. It's helpful if you rode slowly at first, avoiding a lot of turns and twists. It's also useful if you always keep your dog on a leash, so consider getting a bicycle attachment so that you won't need to hold the leash.

❖ Hiking

A hike with your dog might be the perfect activity for someone who loves nature and dogs. A hike will give your dog a deeper experience of the world than a simple walk. Start out with short hikes on a cooler day when hiking with your dog for the first time. Once your dog has gotten used to easy to moderate hikes and will be more sure-footed, avoid difficult trails.

Ensure that you bring a lot of water. It's even possible for your dog to take its own backpack; make sure it's well-balanced and not too heavy.

Swimming

Not all dogs are capable of swimming, contrary to popular belief. Some dogs dislike swimming. Anyone who has a water dog knows this. Take your dog swimming! You can combine swimming with the game of fetch to make it even more fun. Just be sure to follow these water safety guidelines.

You can still teach your dog to swim if the pup likes the water but cannot swim. Begin with shallow water and a doggie life jacket until it gets the hang of it. If the fur baby likes the water, then it'll likely get comfortable real quick. Don't push the dog into the water if it doesn't like it. It may just be that your dog loves the land!

❧ Games

You can play many fun games with your dog, some of which will also provide some exercise. Dogs get moderate exercise from fetch, hide-and-seek, and tug of war while you get light exercise from them.

It's also possible to use games to train your dog, which is a great way to stimulate his mind.

❧ Dog Sports

Nowadays, there are many exciting dog sports available, and new ones are always popping up. Agility and canine freestyle will give your dog a great workout and offer some light to moderate exercise for you.

Make sure you research the dog sports that might be right for your dog before you get started. After that, look for classes that will teach you and your dog the sport in your area.

Safety First

Please consult your veterinarian before beginning any exercise program for your dog. Let your dog set the pace when exercising with her. Take water and rest breaks from time to time. Dogs with short muzzle, such as a Bulldog or Pug, should avoid exercising in hot temperatures.

Whatever type of dog you have, be on the lookout for signs of exhaustion, illness, or injury. Don't exercise if your pet seems tired or ill. When exercising with your dog, pay attention to your surroundings. It may be dangerous for your dog to be distracted if other dogs or people are around, especially if it's is off-leash.

PART 3

5 STEPS TO GET A PERFECTLY BEHAVED PUPPY.

CHAPTER 7

Step 1: Methods and Principles of Training, Basic Skills

There are as many dog training methods as there are dog breeds.

Ok... I might have exaggerated a little, but you know what I mean.

Various dog training methods will be discussed in this chapter, including their differences. We'll also brush on the basic skills and key principles of dog training.

DOG TRAINING METHODS

As with nearly anything, training your dog involves many methods. For instance, some owners are 100% committed to positive reinforcement and force-free training. In other cases, positive reinforcement may be the predominant strategy, but negative punishment may be used when necessary.

However, others may decide to incorporate positive punishment and negative reinforcement elements, although this isn't recommended and poses serious risks.

Accordingly, the most common methods of dog training are as follows:

1. Alpha/Dominance Dog Training

In alpha dog training, your dog is positioned under you in a "pack structure."

Positive punishment is a key component of dominance training. The best solution for punishing your dog for displaying undesirable behavior is to roll him or her on its back in an alpha roll, which is also called a submissive position.

Training based on the Alpha method also requires setting ground rules, such as guiding your dog through doorways and on walks and only letting him or her eat after you've finished dinner and given it permission to do so. Alpha-based training programs often use vibrating collars or static collars for correction.

Trainers who focus on alpha/dominance may also integrate positive rewards while training. The term "balanced approach" or "balanced training" is often used by trainers who use positive reinforcement and positive punishment together. However, those who think positive punishment poses risks find the term misleading.

Training dominance dogs is heavily based on historical perceptions of pack behavior among wolves, with formative papers by Rudolph

Schenkel in 1947, Expressions Studies on Wolves, and wildlife biologist L. David Mech's 1970 book.

Scientists have demonstrated that most of the supposed wolf-pack dynamics the dominance training style is based on are incorrect. A serious problem with Schenkel's 1947 study is that it shows how ill-conceived the idea of an alpha wolf is.

As a result, we now know:

- Observations on wolves in captivity at a zoo in Switzerland, rather than wild wolves, were made in 1947.
- Researchers have found that wild wolves actually live in family groups, where the "alphas" simply take charge because they are the parents, and there is no dominant competition between them.
- The biologist who coined the term "alpha wolf" has since renounced this term and regrets the publication of his initial book.
- The behavior and social structure of wolves and dogs, despite the fact that they belong to the same species, differ significantly. Their genetic makeup is also completely different.

Although we have said there are many ways to train your dog, we don't recommend alpha/dominance training because it has been scientifically debunked and can severely damage your relationship with your pet. A dog's fear and mistrust are instilled through dominance training, which creates a negative relationship, and has even been shown to increase aggression (after all, dogs display aggressive behaviors when scared).

Having said that, it's not bad to position yourself as a leader to your dog. A truly good leader doesn't use intimidation or fear but instead provides gentle guidance.

PROS

It's sometimes helpful to be your dog's leader. When your puppy looks to you for guidance, you want it to know that you have everything under control. You can do this by being confident you've got things under control. The principals involved in this training philosophy are also useful for teaching manners, such as setting boundaries around doorways and eating.

CONS

Nowadays, most trainers don't recommend dominance training and consider it antiquated. It can not only damage your relationship with your dog, but certain aspects can be dangerous and confusing. Some behavioral problems can also be exacerbated by them, resulting in fear, aggression, anxiety, or bites.

2. Positive Reinforcement Training

The reward-based method, also known as force-free or R+ training, commits strictly to positive reinforcement, using rewards to guide your dog towards desired behaviors.

Modern, science-based dog trainers most often use this type of training. A positive reinforcement concept typically refers to rewarding good behavior with a marker (like a clicker or a marker word like "yes").

Some dogs, however, are more influenced by a favorite toy or simple affection and praise from their owners. It's vital to determine what your dog enjoys and to reward it for good behavior with it.

Rewards might include:

* Any high-value treats (frozen treats, hot dogs, string cheese, etc.)
* Tossing a tennis ball to play fetch
* Using a tug toy to play tug of war
* Butt scratches and pats
* Words of praise and affection.

Positive reinforcement is one of the most versatile approaches to dog training, as it can be used for everything from housebreaking to obedience to agility. Positive training techniques are also likely to be loved by your dog. The benefits of force-free training include:

- ❤ Improved results
- ❤ Raise dogs who enjoy and look forward to training
- ❤ This leads to a stronger bond between you and your dog.

A major downside to using only positive reinforcement is that it requires patience and time. Overall, however, the results are very rewarding as well as safe over time. Teaching your dog new skills through positive reinforcement is the best approach.

Your dog will be motivated and rewarded for good behavior when you use positive training techniques. You must make sure that the reward is equivalent with the task they must complete, such as tasty food. A dog's inherent need and value for food make it a primary reinforcer. Food is a powerful reward for your dog's effort!

Positive reinforcement works in the following way: The more you reward a behavior, the more likely that behavior will recur. Your dog should be able to learn just about anything when you use positive reinforcement correctly!

PROS

Positive reinforcement is popular for a reason, as it strengthens your bond with your pet and promotes a happy training environment. A firm correction, as seen with the alpha approach, can traumatize shy or anxious dogs. It's also easy for your dog to learn since he or she will quickly associate an action with a reward.

CONS

Carrying treats around while positive training can be a hassle. Instead, consider using a treat pouch. It further requires patience and attention to cautiously look for and reinforce good behavior instead of only focusing on bad behavior.

OTHER DOG TRAINING METHODS

1. Clicker Training

Despite being a subset of positive reinforcement training, the clicker technique contains enough information to be worth learning on its own. Training can be done without a clicker - owners can use a marker word (like "yes" or "good") to indicate the desired behavior. It is, however, much more convenient to use a clicker.

The reason for this is that a clicker allows trainers to be much more precise and specific about which behavior the dog is being rewarded for. Clickers also sound the same. It's possible for everyone to use a different tone or intonation when training a dog with a marker word such as "yes," making the marker less effective and not as consistent as it should be.

Here are the basics of clicker training:

❧ Charge your clicker before you use it

This involves teaching the dog to associate clicks with rewards. Do you recall Pavlov's theory of classical conditioning? That's what we're trying to achieve. You'll give your dog a treat with just a click of the clicker at the beginning. All you're doing is creating an association that says "click treat."

❧ Activate desired behavior by clicking

As an example, you might be teaching your dog to sit. If you hold a treat above your dog's head, you might start out by getting it to sit. You'll click and give another treatment as soon as the dog's butt hits the ground.

❧ Repeat as necessary

Continually click and treat your dog until it's reliably sitting without the lure. A pup will learn that sitting results in treats.

❧ Provide a cue

It's now time to pair your action with your cue word (aka command). By saying "sit," you'll be able to click and treat your dog once he or she sits down.

Clicker training is particularly useful when working on complex tricks and agility performance since it's so precise. If your dog is having trouble rolling over, you can break the action down into smaller steps (which can be tough for some dogs).

You can start by clicking and treating your dog just when he or she rolls onto his side, then clicking and treating him when he or she lifts his or her front leg up while lying down, etc. Once you become accustomed to using a clicker, you'll truly be amazed at how your dog will respond.

PROS

It's possible to be extremely precise about which behaviors you reward with clicker training. Tricks and agility training are the most common uses, although behavior training is also great.

CONS

You may experience some difficulty at first with clicker training if you aren't very coordinated. Make things easier by starting slowly and using a sturdy, easy-press clicker. As for deterring existing undesirable behaviors, clicker training isn't very effective.

2. E-Collar Dog Training

E-collars are used for dog training as positive punishment, which involves the use of pain and discomfort to correct unwanted behavior. When a leash cannot be used or when distance training is needed, e-collars are commonly used. When an undesirable behavior is performed, electric shocks, vibrations, or citronella spray can be used as e-training techniques.

There are several serious problems associated with e-training, the biggest being that, while shocking a dog may teach it what behavior it shouldn't do, it does nothing to teach it what it should do instead. It may result in a dog that's too scared to even move because it doesn't know which behavior to perform and is afraid of being punished. Dogs also experience a lot of stress from such training methods.

3. Model-Rival Dog Training

As part of Model-Rival dog training, a dog observes a second dog as it completes the desired behavior and receives a reward for it. The model-rival training method is relatively rare compared to other methods, but it can be useful in certain situations. To drive home the lesson, the model-rival method uses the help of other people or dogs.

Using a cue word, you could instruct one dog to fetch a favorite toy while allowing another to watch.

By demonstrating correct behavior, the dog doing the retrieving serves as a model. Additionally, this other dog serves as a rival - he or she gets to play with the toy instead of having to be trained. You can take advantage of dogs' social nature with this technique.

Researcher Irene Pepperberg first developed the model-rival method for training parrots. A variety of empirical tests with dogs have proved that the method is effective.

PROS

A model-rival can be helpful in expanding your pup's skillset if he or she is learning how to perform a job or provide a service. The training of seeing-eye dogs is particularly helpful here. This might be a fun alternative to obedience training if you're looking for something different.

CONS

Without specialized training, the training won't be helpful with most day-to-day tasks. A lot of repetition and focus are required for trainers as well, which may not be ideal in all settings and for all dogs.

4. Relationship-Based Dog Training

By teaching the pup commands at a level that's easy to understand, relationship-based dog training recognizes that your dog has feelings. During training, your pup should be kept relaxed and happy. In order to raise the difficulty, you'll begin by teaching commands in a distraction-free area. Be patient throughout training and go at your dog's pace.

A relationship-based training approach focuses on understanding your dog as an individual. Examples of relationship-based training include:

* When your dog is stressed or nervous, you can identify those emotions from its body language.
* Consider carefully whether your dog is in an environment that's overstimulating. Does he or she seem tired? Is his or her leg sore?

In positive training, you want to make sure your dog feels confident and comfortable during the process. During relationship-based training, you reward your dog with attention and your relationship rather than treats, toys, or games.

Although some people consider relationship-based training distinct from positive training, others don't.

PROS

Any good dog training session should begin with a relationship-based approach. Training should be tailored to your dog's personality and keep his feelings in mind. It also encourages you to learn the body language of dogs, which is always helpful.

CONS

Training strong-willed dogs can be slow or challenging due to their need for more motivation. You and your dog can easily become distracted in multi-dog situations where this approach isn't ideal.

5. Science-Based Dog Training

An objective of science-based dog training is to use empirical evidence when achieving the desired outcome. In other words, ask, "What does the science say?"

New studies and experiments are continuously being conducted to better understand how our four-legged pals learn. Dog cognition is still a relatively new field.

The goal of science-based training is to evaluate the effectiveness of rewards and punishments and to understand how dogs can be conditioned. Science-based dog training is a difficult concept to define since it's constantly evolving and changing, but it essentially means following the most up-to-date, well-researched training methods available.

In the same way as relationship-based training, many trainers see relationship-based training as more of an attitude or mindset than a specific training approach. In addition, there's a large amount of overlap, as most training approaches use some empirical data to inform the training sessions.

PROS

Owners benefit from learning more about dog behavior by using this approach. By doing this, you ensure that you're totally committed to understanding your dog based on the latest research and science.

CONS

Staying on track with the latest scientific studies about canine behavior can be difficult and time-consuming, which is why only professional trainers and behavior consultants are dedicated to this task.

KEY PRINCIPLES OF DOG TRAINING

Training a dog can be a nightmare if you lack some fundamental understanding of the key principles of dog training. Bear these tips in mind as you train your dog.

Bonding with Your Dog

The bond you form with your dog should be one of your main concerns from the moment you bring her home. Since a dog's exceptional behavior is primarily the result of a strong relationship based on love, respect, and understanding, the behavior is a byproduct.

Research has found that dogs prefer spending time with humans than with their own kennel mates. Fortunately, dogs are hardwired to want to bond with us. It turns out that dogs think we're pretty awesome, too, despite how much we love them. Studies reiterate that both people and dogs experience an increase in oxytocin (the "bonding hormone") during human-animal interactions.

A neuroscientist at Emory University and author of the book, *How Dogs Love Us,* Gregory Berns, MD, PhD, studied the canine brain with MRI technology for years. His research found that dogs and humans experience emotions in a similar way based on brain activity. Playing with your cute dog friend is one of the best ways to bond with it! You establish a bond with most dogs by playing with them, such as playing fetch, tug-of-war, or even chasing them in the backyard.

In Plato's words, "It is easier to discover more about a person in one hour of play than it is in a year of conversation." It certainly applies to dogs as well. You must bond with your dog in order for it to know that he or she can rely on you and trust you. It should have a full water bowl, be fed and walked at regular intervals, and be spoken to in a kind voice. You'll find bonding with dogs is easy when you meet their basic needs and wants.

When my students learn to use the part of their brain that helps them become good parents, they become the best teachers to their dogs.

"Well, parenting a child is very different from parenting a dog." That's true, but they have more in common than you might realize. Dogs tend to interact more in situations they might otherwise be apprehensive in if they have a "secure base"- someone with whom they feel comfortable. As a child might not go to a birthday party without one's parents by his or her side, a hesitant dog might feel more comfortable if you're with it in a new situation. Once the pup feels more comfortable, he or she might be willing to explore. We're not anthropomorphizing dogs in this case; we're using science.

Exercises & Basic Skills

A dog's health depends on maintaining physical activity, but it goes beyond that.

Until the dog has exercised and exhausted some of her energy, you cannot expect it to be able to absorb new concepts and concentrate on the lesson at hand. When your dog exhibits unwanted behavior, such as shredding up furniture every time you leave the house, jumping on guests at the door or digging up the backyard, it's most likely due to a lack of regular mental and physical exercise. Many dogs don't get enough exercise; it's a necessity.

At the start of the 2oth century, dogs actually had a job and performed certain functions, such as hunting and herding, to channel their energy. Dogs are rarely expected to perform many of the tasks they were originally bred to perform, as our culture has changed dramatically. Nevertheless, we should continue to challenge them. Despite the fact that not all Border Collies are bred to herd sheep, I've once had three with every desire and energy to engage in this kind of activity.

Even though I don't have any sheep, I do have Frisbees and balls, so I'm able to offer my dogs an outlet: working with a person to accomplish a physical goal. Although they don't herd sheep, they chase balls and bring them back, and this seems to make them very happy. Dogs, at their core, require a lot of human interaction, and training can be more effective when you combine human interaction with exercise.

Depending on the dog's energy level, walks, a trip to the dog park, and time to run around the yard may suffice. Level three dogs, on the other hand, are full of energy and are always ready to go, so these activities won't be enough. So what will? The best way to satisfy a dog both physically and mentally is to play fetch with him or her.

Fetch

The following information will help you to effectively teach fetch:

- ❧ To begin with, let's make sure we're talking about the same thing when it comes to fetching. It consists of throwing a toy, your dog chasing it, picking it up, bringing it back, and letting it go readily. Rather than retrieving a still object, your dog is chasing a moving object. It's normal for your dog to not learn the game immediately. It can take several weeks. For some two, while others up to 12 weeks.

- ❧ Avoid using treats. Within minutes of using food, teaching your dog to fetch isn't a good idea, as the dog is in food mode and is less likely to grab with his or her mouth. When you play fetch correctly, the reward should be the toy or object you're playing with, not something edible.

- ❧ Play fetch with a toy your dog really enjoys. Try it out and see what works. The first time I got my dog Thunderbolt, he barely cared about playing Frisbee with me. One day, I saw him fascinated by a feather-duster-looking cat toy at a pet supply store. As opposed to thinking, "This isn't a toy for dogs. Let's keep going!" I bought the toy, ripped off the feathers, and taped them to the Frisbee. Having played fetch with the Frisbee ever since Thunderbolt has played before hundreds of thousands of people in Frisbee shows. Try different toys. Consider a rope toy first, and if that doesn't work, try something else.

🐾 Please don't throw items at your dog and expect them to run after them. Get her really excited about it first. Make up a game of keep-away with the toy or pretend that you're playing with it yourself and having a lot of fun. Your goal is to make your dog want to grab it.

🐾 Tie the item in a tug-of-war. This is an important step in teaching fetch. It's a good sign that your dog loves tug-of-war with an object and is well on his or her way to learning to fetch when she starts playing with it.

🐾 Let your pup go off with the toy if you're teaching him or her to like it. If you're teaching your dog to like a toy, then you must make it uninteresting to hold on to it. Make sure you hold the toy firmly in your hand, as though it's in a vice. Also, act bored and uncaring as though you couldn't care less whether your dog pulls on the toy. Be sure not to look at him her, and be sure not to move the toy.

- 🐾 We may need a few minutes or seconds to complete this process. Patiently wait. When your dog becomes bored with the toy and lets go of it, tell her "Yes!" and give her the toy back as a reward for proper behavior. It's common for people to delay rewarding these critical successes with a toy for too long. Avoid this mistake at all costs. This tells him or her, "You may have the toy if you want, but you have to play by my rules." Stripping it out of one's mouth doesn't teach the pup anything and isn't a long-term solution for most dogs.

- 🐾 Toss the toy a few feet away; the number of repetitions is more important at this point. Run alongside your dog but slightly behind it to avoid distracting from the moving toy while the pup runs after it. It might be necessary to point to the toy or nudge it a bit if your dog doesn't pick up the toy at first. Get eye contact with your dog after he or she picks up the toy, then bolt back to the point of origin, and make your dog chase you.

Dogs that are energetic love to chase, and your insistence that yours do the same reinforces this behavior. The first two components to teaching fetch are tug-of-war and "let go," and the third is chasing after the toy. Once you have that down pat, run halfway with your dog and encourage her to keep following. You eventually won't have to run at all once you've covered 25 % of the distance.

Learning to Communicate

As soon as you begin training your dog, you need to establish some basic communication. Most known living creatures aren't hardwired for that, but dogs are. *The Genius of Dogs* author Brian Hare once said, "Of all the species on this planet, dogs are the only ones with the ability to read intentions and understand what is being communicated. Our closest relatives, chimpanzees and bonobos, don't possess it. Dogs are actually capable of understanding us in a way that some species cannot."

It may take some time to establish mutual communication with a puppy or a newly acquired dog without much training. As you're building communication, it's important to control the environment so that your dog knows what it's supposed to do. Don't give up—it might seem like this process is taking longer than it should. Laying some groundwork can take a week or two. Once you've done that, things will move much more quickly.

To effectively communicate with your dog, you'll need to know these basics:

❧ Eye Contact

Communication can be greatly enhanced by eye contact. When dogs look at us, they're gathering information about how we're feeling, when and where they'll get fed, or what's going on in a particular situation. In addition to following our gaze, dogs are also capable of understanding its meaning.

You don't have to stare your dog down; it's just a matter of looking at her as you would another human being. In teaching your dog eye contact at first, being aware of the training bubble - the distance between your eyes and its - will go a long way: the closer your eyes are to the pups, the faster he or she will likely respond. It's even recommended that you sit on the ground when teaching your dog at first so that you can really see eye-to-eye with the pup. As time goes on, the bubble between you and the other person can "stretch." Be careful, though, or you'll burst it.

❧ Hand Signals

Imagine communicating with someone who doesn't speak your language using a lot of hand signals at first. That's what dogs do, too. At first, they might not understand what we're saying, and they'll never understand everything we say, but hand signals and body language help them understand our intentions.

I use exaggerated body language, gestures, and pointing when teaching dogs, in addition to using words and encouraging them. You may find that some dogs respond more to hand signals than words, or vice versa, but be sure to incorporate a lot of body language in the beginning. You don't have to use standard hand signals. There's no denying that dogs are able to understand our hand signals better than any other species.

Hare and other researchers found, for instance, that if you placed a treat under one of two cups and pointed to it or gazed at it, a dog was more likely to go toward the correct cup than a chimpanzee. It has been proven that dogs don't just rely on their sense of smell to find food but follow gestures from humans to find the right cup.

This implies that dogs are able to understand human communication in a way that chimpanzees cannot, says Dr. Hare. The way dogs understand human gestures in an intuitive way is truly remarkable.

🐾 Teaching Your Language

When it comes to understanding us, the average dog's vocabulary is comparable to a young child's, so don't hold back when you teach your language. It's key for you to link certain words to specific actions. As an example, let's take "down." Just say it once instead of "Down, down, down, down."

In addition, repeating a word more than once might cause your dog to interpret it as "down down down down." Once your dog sees that you're repeating "down" four times, she may use that as a precedent to regularly wait until you reach the fourth request.

As an exception, sometimes you may give a command like "down." You can do that again to allow your dog remain in a fixed position for a few more seconds. However, keep your command short and simple.

Simply withhold the reward if your dog doesn't do what you've taught her. Furthermore, it can take a few weeks to teach basic vocabulary. The word needs to be said after the dog performs the skill when teaching a new word. Use a lure and hand signals to get your dog into a down position, as an example. After giving him or her a treat, say "Down!" slowly, once at a normal volume, and with purpose.

Learning Your Dog's Communication Cues

Our dogs need to learn to understand us, but we need to learn to comprehend them as well. There is no one-way street in a relationship! Any dog owner knows that a dog's barks, growls, whines, and other expressions mean something different. I'll wager that you can distinguish a bark that indicates a stranger is approaching from a playful bark or one that reveals hunger.

As with us, dogs communicate their feelings through their body language. Certain dog postures and movements are helpful for telling the difference between a growl that says "Let's play!" and one that suggests, "Back away." For instance, some dogs can stand still like a statue with eyes closed and mouth closed. This might seem aggressive to outsiders. However, it might mean, "Please, I'll do anything if you'll just throw a toy for me right now."

Everything depends on context. Pay attention to these cues:

❧ Tail

The dog's upright posture usually indicates interest; if it's wagging side to side in conjunction with another body language, which appears to indicate happiness, then it's probably excited or trying to play. The dog's tail tucked between its legs could suggest fear and anxiety, while slow, deliberate wags could imply uncertainty.

❧ Ears

These are probably pulled back when a dog is fearful or anxious, relaxed, or just listening to the world around her, whereas when they're pricked forward, the dog is probably very alert or highly interested in something.

❧ Eyes

You'll be able to tell what your dog is thinking by looking into his or her eyes as you become more familiar with your fur baby. You may notice dilated pupils, darting eyes from side to side, or the whites of one's eyes if fearful. You may feel threatened when someone stares directly at you with an intense stare, but there are exceptions to this rule.

❧ Mouth

The mouths of scared dogs may be closed, as well as their teeth bared and lips curled. Dogs that are anxious pant and lick their lips frequently. Dogs whose mouths are open and their tongues out maybe playful or relaxed (but if they're panting, it could mean they're uneasy or overheated).

❧ Posture

Dogs that are timid or afraid may crouch low to the ground, while those who are confident may stand tall. It probably means they're easygoing in that setting if they seem natural and relaxed.

Be Consistent

A dog trainer who's truly successful is consistent. You'll probably be unable to understand your dog in the way that you would. I cannot stress this enough. Consistency requires some effort, but it isn't that difficult.

If your dog doesn't come when you ask him or her to "come," then it's on you to shift into training mode for a few seconds or minutes and motivate the pup to come, no matter what you're doing. Now that you've given the request, follow it through to the end to ensure that you get the results you want. Consistency may require you to get a treat and lure your dog every step of the way from where you called or possibly escort it on a leash, but this is what it means to be steady.

Additionally, if you don't like something, then it's your responsibility to prevent it from happening again. It takes longer to resolve every instance in which your dog does something you don't want. You don't call your dog back and repeat this training exercise after he or she runs into another room after being asked to stay.

There has been a mistake in your consistency, which may eventually lead to a dog that listens and responds only occasionally. It's important to divert your puppy's attention to something else that he or she can chew on whenever you notice that your puppy is chewing on the table leg. If you follow the troubleshooting section on chewing, you'll get great results. In a nutshell, be relentlessly consistent, and you'll see amazing outcomes.

Control the Environment

Providing their dogs with too much freedom too soon by not controlling their environment is the number one mistake that new pet parents make! Training your dog effectively requires you to control its environment. You can't just wing it-dogs are very intelligent, but they don't know how to interact in our culture without our guidance.

To make sure my dog is with me when I get up to go to the kitchen, check the mail, or do yard work; I attach a four- to six-foot leash to my belt loop. This will reduce how your dog asks about the expensive shoes you left by the front door, but it'll give you a chance to avoid or interrupt potential behaviors you don't wish to repeat. Additionally, it delivers more opportunities to see your dog do things you like, so you can reiterate how much you like him or her.

When training your dog, keep your pup attached to you or in a puppy-proofed area for the first few weeks or months. This will prevent bad habits from forming. When you don't want your dog to do something, you need to put it in a setting where the dog cannot do it.

Train from the Inside Out

The best way to achieve long-term results with your dog is not to force your dog into doing something (which I call "outside-in training"), but to make your dog want to do something (called "inside-out training").

With outside-in training, the idea is to make your dog's life temporarily unpleasant in order to discourage certain behaviors. In my opinion, this is a less-than-ideal strategy known as "experiential avoidance." According to traditional dog trainers, outside influences - such as leash jerking, manhandling, or devices such as choke chains or prong collars - are used to correct behavior so that the dog understands "Don't do that."

Some trainers actually take advantage of the dog misbehaving or messing up so they can teach her a lesson. This is a dated, amateurish approach. In fact, we can communicate much more intelligently with dogs than this. Outside-in training poses a number of problems. Firstly, it doesn't promote the bond between a person and a dog, which is an integral part of training. The mere fact that this type of training is offered to the public should be grounds for dismissal. If you can't both enjoy teaching a dog, then there's no point in doing so.

Not only do I respect my dogs, but I also know that this is how they learn best. I want the dogs I train to be buzzing and loving life to the fullest. In addition, outside-in training rarely, if ever, produces long-term results, as I explain in this chapter. Forces such as pushing a dog's back into a sit position - even if simple and benign - don't teach your dog in a way that encourages him or her to think for itself. A dog is simply too complex an animal to be taught this way.

Although I'm not advocating touching your dog during training, if he or she ever needs assistance getting out of the pool, you should certainly help your pup! To get the best results, you shouldn't rely on physically controlling it as a primary training strategy. Our dogs' sophisticated brains benefit from inside-out training, on the other hand. If they're taught to behave a certain way by you, and they think for themselves, then more likely than not, they'll repeat that behavior on their own. Moreover, you'll see results much faster, and your dog will be better prepared for the years to come.

What is the best way to get your dog to think from the inside out? In addition to bonding and communicating with your dog, you have to show your dog the right thing to do and then reward with a treat and/or playtime as well as genuine praise.

If you were a child and an authority figure gave you sincere praise, how did you feel? It's possible that you aced a test, and your teacher announced that you had the highest grade in the class. There's a good chance you tried extra hard to repeat your performance. The more my parents and teachers praised me and recognized my achievements, the faster I advanced as a child.

That's what we want from our dogs. Additionally, inside-out training addresses the cause of a problem, not its symptoms. Using bitter-tasting sprays won't stop your dog from chewing a table leg, for instance. The spray may help him or she to avoid that table leg until it wears off, but he or she hasn't learned how to chew up your house and possessions. These types of tools are just bandages, and they don't cure the problem (which in the case of chewing is probably boredom or teething). All of what I'll teach will be aimed at addressing the cause, and this will make all the difference.

CHAPTER 8

Step 2: Obedience, First Commands

What could be better than having a cute puppy?

Having an obedient puppy!

Dogs are often portrayed as very obedient and dutiful. But not in all cases. I've worked with crazy dogs who would never sit when you say so. If you have a similar experience with your dog, then you might want to read in between the lines of this chapter. Here I'll describe different basic commands and how you can get your dog to obey them.

Let's start with leash training.

OBEDIENCE AND LEASH TRAINING

It'll usually take up to three weeks to six months for your dog to master leash walking, depending on your consistency and your dog's energy. It takes more than just sitting and staying. While some dogs can enjoy a leisurely walk, others require more assistance. When you ask your dog to walk slowly, you're requesting it to do something that's highly unnatural. Be sympathetic!

As compared to the four-legged variety, humans are relatively slow-moving mammals. Leash training shouldn't be attempted during regular walks or training sessions. They should be separated. I cannot emphasize more how essential for you to care for your pet's physical and mental needs before beginning leash walking training. It's unreasonable to expect dogs to understand intricate concepts like walking more slowly next to a person until you can exhaust their overflowing energy with a game of fetch or another activity.

Here are the steps you should take:

1. Introduce this concept inside your house, as you should do with any new concept. If you think that your dog is about to start speeding up or pulling as you begin to walk with it on a leash, stop right away. Getting rid of unwanted behaviors is best done before they happen. Ensure that your dog is looking as soon as you start walking in the opposite direction. If possible, you might even want to walk backward to emphasize making eye contact.

2. Keep rewarding your dog for looking at you repeatedly throughout the lesson. Although you won't expect your dog to stare at you constantly on a leash, you want to make sure she does look at you reliably when you ask her to in this scenario before moving on. Try to keep her enthusiastic about the training session by asking him or her to sit a few times. Because you're now asking your dog to do these easy things with a major variation,

a leash, you should also reward it. During leash training, your main goal should be to have longer periods of time without tension on the leash. Repeat this drill indoors until the dog walks consistently without pulling on the leash.

3. After your dog has been outside for a while, keep it close to home. Take your dog for a walk up and down the street. Due to the distractions, you'll have to slow down your training a little here. In this case, it's simply being outside that's distracting you. At first, be empathetic and let your dog sniff around and take in the world. You can reward your dog heavily whenever he or she walks without tension on the leash and say something like, "You rock!" Remember that a treat doesn't have to be the reward for a good job. I once worked with a high-drive German Shepherd named Venus, who learned to walk on a leash excellently by using tug-of-war as the reward. During the game, he was so high-spirited that he was completely focused on me and not the distractions around him. The session was one of my favorites ever!

4. Stop in your tracks whenever your dog starts pulling or even seems to be pulling forward. If you say "no," state, "It's the pulling that's causing this next action," then abruptly change directions. Try being overly animated or putting a treat at your

dog's nose to get her attention. You'll notice that your dog will glance at you every now and then without you asking for it. When your dog voluntarily does something like this, it's really special, and you should find ways to convey your gratitude. Give the dog a jackpot reward!

5. We went over distraction training earlier, but now you'll be teaching your dog to listen to distractions during leash training. You should test for teachability when you encounter a distraction while walking. In order to prevent this, ask your dog to "sit" periodically as you get further and farther away from the distraction. When the pup sits, he or she is probably in the teachable territory. Your goal now is to get his or her eyes on you and advance extremely slowly, using rewards liberally, and taking small steps backwards as needed.

At about 10 feet or a block away, you may need to back off from the distraction. You may have to go out of sight and work up to very distracting scenarios in more severe cases. Dogs cannot be taught to look at you or sit if they refuse to look at you or sit. Perhaps it's just not the right time for your dog to look at you or sit. Don't give up!

Over time, you'll need to gradually get the hang of it.

GETTING USED TO LITTER BOX

You might want to train your large dog to use an indoor litter box for a number of reasons. Many dog owners are gone for long periods and don't want to risk even their biggest fur baby having an indoor accident. Having an accident inside could make your adult dog feel punished. Most pups find it easy to take a pee in a litter box while you're away from the house. As a result, he or she can go potty and keep a clean house while staying out of trouble. Don't worry about having a large litter box for your dog if you know you'll be gone for a long time.

Following the steps below will help you teach your dog how to use a litter box or fake grass potty area. Once your dog uses the papers or pads two times, you can move on to the next step.

* Cover the floor inside the area with newspaper or potty pads and set up an exercise pen. To practice over the weekend, give your dog broth to drink to get lots of repetitions.

* Get a timer that will ring every half an hour, and then crate your dog for 5 minutes in a pen. Afterwards, let him or her out. Give a big treat, and then let your pup roam for 30 minutes. If he or she doesn't "go, "then put it back in the crate for another 30 minutes. Repeat as necessary.

- Keep feeding your dog broth. You can reduce the size of the papers or pads once your dog potties reliably on them.
- During the potty time, move the papers or pads into the final potty area or "litter box."
- Now that your dog has become comfortable using the potty area, you can leave the exercise pen door open, and after taking him or her out of the crate, let the dog go in alone to the potty. You're now nearly there!
- Release your dog from the crate and then remove the exercise pen, so that you can encourage it to go potty in the potty area.
- Place the potty area in its final location and work on getting your dog to use it there.

You can remove the crate once your dog is using the potty area and "going" with your guidance (being sure to reward any positive breakthroughs). At this point, male wraps may be an effective preventive measure for your male dogs. If your dog goes potty in areas in the house that are far away from his potty area, you may need to encourage him to go there. Once your dog has used the litter box/potty area for a few weeks, continue rewarding him. The amount of freedom your dog has should be decreased if there are any accidents. By confining your dog to a crate, pen, or indoor tether, you can reduce its freedom.

REST FOR YOUR DOG

While puppies are energetic little bundles of energy, they sleep 18-20 hours a day. In a matter of seconds, your puppy may be a mini-tornado, and in the next, he may fall asleep, almost mid-dash. Healthy growth depends on sleep, which contributes to the development of his central nervous system, brain, immune system, and muscles. Sleep also keeps him or her refreshed during growth spurts.

Puppies burn a lot of energy when they're awake - growing physically, exploring new places and people, learning what they can and cannot do. It's often difficult for them to keep up with their internal clock because the world is such an exciting, stimulating place. Following a few simple guidelines for naps during the day and bedtime can help.

How to Help Your Puppy Sleep During the Day

Don't disturb your puppy. If you let him or her fall asleep in your lap, I'm sure it'll be hard to resist the temptation to cradle the pup, but you don't want it to become dependent on you. You should teach your family members to leave your puppy alone when he or she is sleeping. However, keep an eye on the dog since it'll need to be taken outside upon awakening.

Make sure your puppy knows where to sleep. He or she can nap in his crate, dog bed, or in a quiet place in the house if the pup seems drowsy. Eventually, your fur baby recognize that spot as its sleeping place, even if it takes some time to get the idea.

Maintain a schedule. Schedule his or her day so that active time is followed by quiet time for sleep. After playtime or a walk, the dog will probably be ready for a nap. The napping time may vary from 30 minutes to as long as two hours for your puppy.

Recognize and respond to overtired behavior. Keep him or her from becoming overtired regardless of how much fun you're having. Being overstimulated and overtired can lead to unfortunate behavior. Encourage him or her to wind down by taking it to the crate or a cozy sleeping place.

How to Help Your Puppy Sleep at Night

Create an inviting crate. A new puppy will chew up an expensive bed, so don't buy one. Put two or three soft, inexpensive blankets inside the crate's bottom. Beware of chewing through wool blankets and mats that can result in choking hazards. Make sure to keep a soft toy or blanket in the crate that smells like the pup's mother. In many homes, the puppy's crate is placed in the owner's bedroom so that it can feel like its family is nearby.

Organize your bedtime routine. Your routine will help the dog to learn that nighttime is for sleeping, so you both get a better night's sleep. The pup shouldn't be given any food or water for several hours before going to bed. Play with it, let the animal relieve itself outside, and then give your fur baby a cuddle.

Make sure the dog's sleep area is quiet and dim. Keep the volume and light low if you watch TV in bed. Blackout shades may even be necessary if the room receives early morning light. He or she will know it's time to sleep when it's quiet and dark.

Wire crates can be covered with a cover to make them darker and more den-like. At bedtime, don't give in. Ensure that your puppy gets plenty of physical and mental exercise during the day and that he/she goes to the bathroom. Award with a treat him when the dog gets into its crate to teach him or her to love it. You can expect some whining, barking, and howling before he or she settles in for the night while learning the routine.

Prepare yourself for interruptions. Sometimes puppies, like humans, aren't yet ready to sleep through the night. Your puppy may need to use the bathroom during the night. You'll be able to respond if he or she needs to go out if the dog's sleeping in your bedroom in a crate. Take it outside quietly, praise when he or she goes, and put the dog back in the crate to sleep.

Puppy Sleep Schedule Guide

Routine and structure are essential for puppies. Having a defined sleep, feeding, and house training routine will help you and your puppy adjust to living together. With the help of this sample schedule, you should be able to create a routine that will benefit your canine and human family members.

Morning Puppy Schedule

- During the morning, take the puppy outside to relieve itself as soon as the dog wakes up.
- Serve breakfast to the puppy.
- Dogs usually need a potty break after eating, so give him or her another one.
- Play with the pup, socialize, and take a walk for 30-60 minutes.
- Let him or her sleep. A pup's sleep may last between 30 minutes and two hours.
- When he or she wakes up, let the dog have another potty break.
- Give it lunch.

Afternoon Puppy Schedule

- Give him or her a potty break after lunch.
- Play with your pup and let it explore for up to an hour.
- Time for a nap.
- If he or she needs to go to the bathroom, take the pup outside.
- After that, it's time to play.
- If he or she plays, there's a good chance the dog will settle down for a nap afterwards.
- Take a bathroom break.

Evening Puppy Schedule

- You can give your pup a Kong to play within the crate before you sit down to eat or give dinner before you sit down.
- After dinner, you can take a stroll.

- ❧ He or she can play with family members and interact with them.
- ❧ Ensure that the pup uses the bathroom before bed, and then place into the crate for sleep.

Keep a schedule in mind, but don't let it overwhelm you. Even though it may seem like a lot of work, you'll end up with a happy, well-adjusted dog and enjoy the routine as well. A time like this is ideal for developing a relationship that will last a lifetime.

PREVENTING FOOD AGGRESSION

Dogs, like all pets, can be territorial, especially when it comes to food. Food aggression makes dogs exhibit behaviors such as being protective over their food. Dogs might bite those living with it or could become possessive in other areas. The best way to deal with food aggression in dogs is to properly train them and manage their behavior. There are also ways to prevent it completely.

What's Food Aggression?

Dogs use aggressive behaviors when eating meals or treat to guard their food, which is referred to as food aggression. Many dogs display food aggression. According to one study, almost 20 % of dogs show signs of food aggression.

Aggression is an expression of resource guarding, a behavior passed down through evolution, where dogs guarded every meal or resource they had. However, resource guarding differs somewhat - it refers to a defensive behavior aimed at defending anything they deem valuable, not just food.

Dogs usually guard only what they consider as valuable. Hence, they guard a variety of resources, though food is one of the most common ones.

During mealtime, food can be dropped on the floor, food can be put in the garbage, or even food can be prepared on the counter.

In a household with children, a food-aggressive dog may exhibit this defensive behavior. Younger children often fail to recognize guarding signals and ignore them entirely. If a child grows up in an environment of this type, he or she might be growled at or bitten. Children aren't the only ones at risk from this protective behavior; adults can also be caught in the crossfire. The bottom line is the dog's ability to eat at ease, be comfortable in their environment, and be around people they share their home with.

Causes

Food aggression in dogs isn't caused by one single factor. Among the most common causes are:

- In puppyhood, they can learn by accident or through competition over limited resources in a shelter environment.
- Later in life, dogs may develop food aggression as well. Food aggression can be triggered by trauma, such as the loss of a caretaker, abuse or neglect, or even fighting with another dog. When this occurs, a dog becomes protective over their belongings, especially their food.
- Breeds with dominant or aggressive tendencies may guard food as a consequence of their pack mentality. Hereditary guarding instincts are common in breeds such as English Springer Spaniels, German Shepherds or Rottweilers, though these instincts tend to apply to livestock or property rather than humans.
- While food aggression can have a number of causes, dogs that have spent time in a shelter may be more likely to exhibit this behavior due to competition over available resources like beds, treats, potential mates, and meals.

Signs of Aggression

Food aggression is characterized by several identifying signs, which are categorized according to their harmfulness: mild, moderate and severe.

The best way to identify mild food aggression is through verbal cues. While eating, your dog may growl when you approach one's food. If you raise your arms in warning, your dog may also display its teeth.

A dog with moderate food aggression will snap or lunge when approached by a person or another dog. Dogs that exhibit severe food aggression will bite or chase away the perceived threat.

How to Stop Your Dog's Food Aggression

You can manage this defensive behavior if your dog exhibits some of these signs.

The first thing you should do is spay or neuter your dog. Aggression can be caused by hormones, and spaying or neutering can reduce this tendency.

Training can also be used to treat food aggression: many dogs who display food aggression can go through a seven-stage training program designed to desensitize and counter-condition them to eat near people. Here are seven steps to stop your dog's food aggression:

1. Become familiar with your dog's presence when it eats

Using this step, you'll easily acquaint your dog with the fact that you are present when they are eating meals or treats. While your dog eats food from a bowl on the floor, keep a few feet distance from him. The goal of this training method is for your dog to eat t0 consecutive meals in a relaxed manner before progressing to the next phase.

2. Put a tasty treat in front of you, and then step back

Add a tasty treat to their bowl after the first step, and step back to your original distance following that. Maintain consistency throughout. Make it a goal to make one step forward each day.

3. Talk to your dog while standing close

Close proximity and conversation are the focus of this step. Give your dog a special treat while they're eating from their bowl. Talk in a conversational tone - "What are you eating?" Or simply ask about the dog's food.

Walk away from your dog after giving it the treat. Keep doing this every few seconds. You can move on to the next step of this training process when your dog is relaxed while eating for 10 meals in a row.

4. Feed yourself with your hands

At this stage, hand feeding is a big part of the process. If you feed your dog, it's very important for them to understand that you aren't threatening its food. Talk in a conversational tone with your pup, as you did in the last step. Hold a treat out to your dog while standing next to the bowl. You should encourage your dog to take the treat from your hand, rather than placing it in their bowl.

If they take the treat, walk away and let them know that you aren't interested in their food. Try to lower yourself each day so that your hand is right next to their bowl when they take the treat. Next, after 10 relaxed meals, you can move on to the next step.

5. Touch their bowl without taking food from it

As in the last stage, stay nearby your dog after he has taken the treat from you this time.

Give a treat with one hand and speak in a casual tone. Touch the bowl with the other hand, but don't take food. You can do this so that your dog becomes accustomed to your presence during mealtime. The next phase of training should begin when your dog remains relaxed while eating for 10 consecutive meals.

6. Give them their treat by lifting their bowl off the ground

As you'll be picking their bowl up from the ground to give them a treat, it's vital to build trust during this phase.

Pick up your dog's bowl while speaking calmly to them. Start by lifting the bowl no more than 6-12 inches from the ground, add the treat, and then place it back down. Every day, you'll aim to raise the bowl higher until it can be placed on a table to be prepared. You should repeat this process until you're able to walk a short distance and return your dog's bowl to the same location from which you picked it up.

By the end of this step, you and your dog should have developed trust, and it should be completely comfortable eating around you.

7. Continue the feeding process with the rest of the family

Lastly, repeat steps 1 through 6 with all family members. When your dog begins to trust you with their food, their food aggression should begin to wane or cease entirely.

Your dog may feel comfortable eating around you, but not around other members of your family or guests visiting your home. Consider making your pup's eating environment as safe as possible. Separate bowls for each pet, a gated area for your pup to eat in, or keeping them apart for meal times are all examples of this.

It's common for dogs to just want to feel comfortable while eating a meal. If you're having trouble treating food aggression, you can always consult your vet or a local trainer.

CHAPTER 9

Step 3: Problems and Solutions

A single dog comes with tons of problems. Two dogs are twice the trouble. Three or more? Just be prepared for serious frustration.

Due to their mental and physical state, there are several issues that are associated with dogs. In this chapter, I'll introduce some of the most prevalent problems dogs and dog owners' experience, as well as the best ways to deal with them.

1. Urination

Every dog owner knows that accidents happen. The problem is that your adult dog constantly pees in the house, and it can be very annoying. Please, tackle inappropriate urination as soon as possible. Identifying why your dog pees in the house is the first step. Dogs exhibit inappropriate urinary behavior for a variety of reasons.

Peeping in the house is often called "inappropriate urination" by veterinarians, but it's typically addressed during puppyhood. When your dog is still a puppy, house training might not be complete. There can be a lot of steps in house training, so you may need to revisit them throughout.

There are other reasons for inappropriate peeing if your dog is housetrained; and it they likely began after it was housetrained. A health problem must be ruled out before determining the cause of inappropriate urination.

Your housetrained dog may start peeing in the house again due to a variety of reasons, including urinary tract issues, urinary incontinence, aging problems, or other behavioral issues.

How to handle the behavior:

Never give up on your dog, no matter what you do. You can do it! However, you might need some additional assistance. Until then, be patient with your dog and try one or more simple actions to help it with its problems.

- ❧ Previously house-trained dogs can revisit the training process and repeat the steps.
- ❧ Get your dog outside to pee right after he or she drinks, eats, and wakes up from a nap. Make sure the dog is rewarded for peeing outside where it belongs.
- ❧ Find out if there's a trigger or stimulus in your dog's environment that urges it to pee inside. You can calm your dog's anxiety by changing any element you can. If possible, eliminate the trigger, teach your dog to live with it, or teach your dog to cope with it. While taking walks, avoid sources of fear, such as the aggressive dog in the neighborhood or the jackhammering in progress. Consider playing music or using a white noise machine inside if there are loud noises outside.
- ❧ When your dog urinates in the house, don't hit or yell. It's likely that this will backfire,

and instead of learning that urinating in the house isn't acceptable, your dog may learn that its people are unpredictable or unsafe to be around. If you punish your dog, it may become afraid to urinate in front of you (even outside), which could result in more indoor accidents.

🐾 As soon as possible, remove the odor from each accident by using enzymatic cleaners. The last thing you want is for your dog to think that urinating indoors is acceptable.

🐾 If you're still unable to solve your dog's problem, consider getting a dog trainer or behaviorist involved for an initial consultation or more frequent sessions, as needed.

2. Barking

Dogs bark as a way to communicate -- it's one of the most natural things they do. Barking can be interpreted as showing excitement, happiness, fear, anxiety, suspicion, and many other emotions. When your dog barks, he or she may be alerting you to someone approaching or may be anxious during thunderstorms. Dogs bark out of habit when something outside or far away excites them or when bored.

How to handle the behavior:

Within a few weeks, you should be able to resolve barking issues. In addition to making sure your dog gets enough exercise, you can try the following:

* ❧ Organize training exercises instead of waiting for real-life situations to arise. First ask your dog some simple commands like "sit" or "down." Reward them generously. Next, have your dog bark if someone walks back and forth in front of your house, knocks on the door repeatedly, or rings the doorbell. Reward if the dog is quiet. Taking a step back can help your dog calm down; ask your friend to knock once instead of three times or even lightly tap the door to get some traction. Try to find the point at which your dog is willing to comply.
* ❧ Besides the primary sessions, there will also be spontaneous secondary sessions (which may occur more than once a day if your dog is a big barker). Barking is usually preceded by announcing that the dog is going to bark. Whenever your dog sees or hears something outside, his or her ears may prick up, and the fur baby may begin to focus on it. Before he or she barks, this is the best time to train your dog. First, get it to pay attention to you.

This is a perfect way to teach your dog to look at you and to leave it! Initially, things may seem difficult, as your dog may think, "How can I possibly look at you when there is a dog walking in front of our house?" You must aim for small signs of compliance, such as a quick glance in your direction. Immediately acknowledge this little success by saying, "Yes!" and reward him or her.

- If your dog continues to bark despite your efforts and you cannot get its attention, move him or her away from the distraction. The pup may need to be escorted to a bedroom where it can fully concentrate. Then you can move to the hallway and work your way closer to the door once you've perfected this. No matter whether outside distractions have disappeared, it's still vital to carry out this impromptu training session. Praise and reward quiet behavior.

- You won't be around to train your dog if he or she barks while you're away from the house. Ensure your dog is exercised and placed in a part of the house where it won't bark, such as away from a window with a view of the sidewalk. So the pup will be more likely to stay on track regardless of your presence.

- Don't forget that barking doesn't have to be all or nothing. Dogs sometimes bark once or twice to alert their owners to what's happening outside. Then simply wait until after the first or second bark to get your dog's attention and follow the previous instructions.

3. Nausea in the car

The process of desensitizing or counter-conditioning your dog to car travel may take some time, but it's not impossible. With the help of a trained dog behaviorist, you'll be able to take your dog on more trips and spend more time with him or her.

It's best to take several short trips before a long trip to ease a dog's travel anxiety. Get your dog in the car, start the engine, and sit there for a few minutes without moving. Continue this process the following day, but back out of your driveway before returning. If your dog behaves well, be sure to praise and reward the pup with food. If that doesn't work, try walking around the block. Gradually increase your riding time until you're totally comfortable for 20 to 30 minutes.

It might take a few days or even weeks for your dog to adjust to riding in the car comfortably. Your nervous pet should be gradually exposed to more challenging stimuli over time. It isn't possible to force your dog to "get over" or "deal with" one's anxiety. Dogs can be scared to travel in a motor vehicle, and he/she needs time to adjust. If your dog starts to howl or whine, keep calm and don't scold him. Visible anxiety is a sign that training should be halted and restarted the following day. If you continue to expose your dog to stressful situations, the animal will further associate the car with fear and displeasure, setting back your training efforts. Travelling in an airplane or train can also be practiced in a car carrier.

How to handle the behavior:

You can make your dog's travel more enjoyable and reduce motion sickness by following these tips:

- Before travelling, you shouldn't give your dog food 12 hours before. It is best to travel on an empty stomach in order to reduce nausea and the need for frequent potty breaks, especially on long car rides or when travelling by plane or train. Fresh water should always be readily available. Owners can hang water bottles on the carrier doors to keep pets hydrated.
- Dog safety harnesses and carriers are also recommended. Anxious dogs are prone to harming themselves, as well as to causing accidents. Many dogs consider carriers as a "safe place."

- ❧ It's important to keep the car cool and quiet. Maintain cool temperatures and play soft, classical music.
- ❧ Include the smell of home as well. Put your scent on a blanket or t-shirt and place it in your dog's carrier. Nothing is cozier than mom or dad's shirt, aside from the fact that it smells like home.
- ❧ You should bring special toys on your trip. Playing with new toys during travel can help your dog associate travel with fun.

4. Eating feces and chewing things

Despite what some people think, this is a very common behavior called "coprophagia," Greek for "eating feces." Many dogs will eat their own poop or the poop of other animals for no apparent reason. It's possible for dogs to eat their own feces in order to clean the nest or to do it as a way to encourage their offspring to eliminate (female dogs will often lick their puppies' backsides to encourage them to eliminate).

According to my observations, coprophagia is more common in dogs under 18 months old. Yet this behavior needs to be stopped regardless of its cause. To be blunt, it's very disgusting. Additionally, your dog can get intestinal parasites or other bacteria if he or she eats another animal's wastes. Dogs can also transfer such bacteria to humans if they eat poop, especially if they love to kiss a lot. If your pet is suffering from coprophagia, speak to your veterinarian to rule out medical causes.

However, other than that, if you leave your dog unattended or don't control its environment, your dog can get away with this behavior. The only way to stop your dog from engaging in the behavior is to interrupt it, grab its attention, and leave a treat when the pup obeys. It's just another way to say "leave it" to food and chewable goods you don't want to be consumed.

Coprophagia normally outgrows in most dogs, but to end it sooner rather than later, supervise carefully when your dog is outside and pick up its waste right away. Immediately after your dog goes poo, give a treat so that the fur baby will look forward to the treat, rather than the one left behind. Dogs like to raid litter boxes because the high protein content in cat food makes cat poop very appealing to them, so it's important to restrict access by either putting them behind a cat door (assuming your dog cannot fit through it) or raising them high enough so that only they can access them.

Puppy teething causes them to chew because their teeth are coming in (just like that for human babies), and gnawing on things helps relieve that pain. The reasons for older dogs chewing vary: either they were never taught how to chew like puppies, or they're bored and chew to keep themselves occupied. Dogs love to explore the world around them. It's logical that puppies use their mouths to check things out since their sense of taste and feeling is the first to develop (dogs are born blind and deaf!), says Dr. Herron.

Chewing is also instinctual-dogs chewed and ground bone and marrow thousands of years ago to survive, and they still exhibit this behavior today. It doesn't matter why your dog chews. You can help stop no matter how old the dog is. It's important to know that dogs may chew when they're scared or anxious. In that case, if you want to stop chewing, you must address those causes specifically.

How to handle the behavior:

- ❀ Supervise your dog or otherwise contain him, he or she cannot chew up your couch or tear apart your favorite shoes. Even if the dog is five years old, take total control of his or her surroundings and go back to basics. If you want to solve this problem, it's paramount that you do that.
- ❀ Also, understand that in many cases, especially if your dog is teething, you shouldn't prevent him or her from chewing.

You should instead make sure he knows what to chew on. Provide a variety of durable and safe toys of various textures around the house, such as bones and antlers.

🐾 Try to experiment a bit. For example, if you notice your dog wandering over to your shoe and gnawing on it, do all you can to get its attention. If that doesn't work, try clapping your hands or getting super-animated to distract it for a moment.

🐾 You shouldn't grab the dog or the shoe at this point. You want the animal to initiate restraint (remember, inside out!). As soon as you have its attention, state a sincere "Yes!" and offer a chew toy of comparable texture to satisfy it. You can even play with the toy a little bit. As a result, your dog knows two things: "I have a chew toy over here, and listening to me makes your life more interesting." Next time, keep your shoes (or anything else your dog might destroy) out of reach.

🐾 Last but not least, play with your dog as much as possible. If he or she feels content instead of chewing apart everything he finds, maybe next time, the dog will take a nap or just feel better! Gimmicks such as chew-deterrent sprays attempt to suppress the behavior rather than tackle the underlying causes. Don't just tell your dog to avoid items because of a bad-tasting spray. Teach it to understand you, as well as think for itself.

5. Jumping

A dog's natural instinct is to jump on people. Their primary motivation is to interact with you near your face. The only problem is, because humans are taller than dogs, the animals must jump up to reach. Traditional trainers may tell you that dogs jump on people to dominate us, but this is simply not true. You haven't yet taught your dog not to jump when he or she sees you or people visiting your home because the pup is really excited to see them. In addition, mellow dogs seldom jump excessively-it's the high-energy ones who have a hard time keeping all four paws on the ground. Keeping them on the ground will require some extra patience.

How to handle the behavior:

As part of chapter 11, I cover proper greetings as part of basic training because this is such a common issue. Keep reading to chapter 11 to teach your dog this skill if he or she jumps.

6. Digging

Digging may occur for a variety of reasons; dogs may uncover dirt as a way of cooling off if the atmosphere outside is too hot. Sometimes, dogs dig up yards because they're energetic and bored.

How to handle the behavior:

Bringing your dog inside will help him or her to stay cool if, of course, he or she digs holes just to stay cool. Aside from that, I cannot recall an instance where regular, sufficient exercise didn't resolve this issue. Play with your dog and teach plenty of tricks as well as offer some suitable toys. Your dog will have to be continuously supervised while outside if you're unable to exercise it.

7. Hyperactivity

No happy dog would suddenly start spinning in circles, jumping up and down, or barking and yipping. Excessive excitement is the sign of a happy dog. It's only through physical activity that his or her brain knows how to deal with the excess energy.

These signs are often interpreted as happiness by people. Additionally, many people find it cute when a dog behaves in this way and wind up unknowingly enabling the behavior. You'll prevent future misbehaviors, such as aggression, by curbing your dog's excitement. Excited dogs are not happy dogs. Calm dogs are. Here's how you can get your dog from being constantly over-excited to being calm, submissive, and happy.

How to handle the behavior:

❧ Keep Excitement to a Minimum

What you do when your dog approaches you with excitement will determine how often such behavior occurs. Giving affection or attention to an excited dog is the worst thing you can do. You're merely expressing your joy at his actions. Being excited will earn him or her a reward, so the dog will keep doing it. If the dog is overly excited, ignore it. Don't talk to it, don't touch it. Try to turn the other way or gently push it back down if he or she jumps on you.

❧ Calmly encourage calm behavior

In this tip, you'll learn the other side of the coin. You can give affection and attention to your dog when it is calm and submissive, which reinforces that state. You should reward your dog when it's calm. You can help your dog naturally and instinctively become calmer by ignoring excited behaviors and rewarding calm behaviors.

❧ Wear Your Dog Out

If your dog doesn't have the energy to do it, it's easier to keep it from becoming overly excited, which is why a walk can be so important. Besides providing directed exercise, it drains your dog's energy while channeling it. It isn't enough to let your dog run around in the yard and do his or her business. Your fur baby may even become more excited after this activity is over, rather than less. Likewise, you shouldn't take your dog for a walk just so it can do its business and go home. As the pack looks for food, water, and shelter together, the movement mimics that of the pack on a mission. By doing so, your dog will stay in touch with one's primal instincts; stay focused on moving forward, and drain any excess energy. If you bring your dog home with excess energy from exercise, he or she will then associate that feeling of calm with this reward.

❧ Allow a limited number of outlets

It's also possible to reduce excessive energy by stimulating your dog's mind. Playtime is a good way to do this. It's a good idea to stimulate your dog's mind and burn off some energy by playing fetch, having him search for hidden treats, or running him through obstacle courses. What's important is that you control how long and how intense the activity is. The key is to set limits. Stop the game if your dog becomes overexcited. It's a form of gentle punishment. By rewarding calm behavior and creating limitations, you're telling your dog, "If I get too crazy, the treat goes away."

❧ Put their noses to work

It has been shown that capturing a dog's sense of smell can have a calming effect, as the nose is her primary sense organ. If you associate scents like lavender and vanilla with times when your dog is calm - like keeping scented air fresheners near her bed - you can help calm your dog down. Before you use a scent, check with your veterinarian to make sure your dog doesn't have allergies to it and ask for recommendations on the best scent to use.

☙ Calm down

Monitor your own energy level if you want your dog to be calm. What do you do when you want your dog to be corrected? Do you scream over every bad thing he or she does? or can you stop his unwanted behavior with a nudge or a quiet word? You're contributing to your dog's excitement if you are in the second category. Using a loud sound to correct your dog is only necessary when the pup is engaging in a dangerous activity, such as running into traffic. To get your dog's attention, you should only need to make that short, sharp sound.

I want you to think about this image: two soldiers in the woods. They've reached a clearing and can see the enemy ahead of them. The first one moves forward. What can the other soldier do? Not by screaming. Perhaps you can picture it in your head - a hand on the shoulder or arm across the chest, without saying a word. As hunters, dogs instinctively understand this kind of correction. If the Pack Leader yelled to tell the group to stop when the group came upon a deer in a clearing, the deer would have long gone, and none of them would eat. Leaders stop the pack with nothing more than their energy and body language.

With these techniques, it can take a while to see results if your dog is naturally high-energy and excitable. Don't give up on them, and be consistent in using them. You can't undo a hyperactive mess overnight since your dog didn't become one overnight. However, you'll be surprised how quickly you'll see a change once you make the commitment. Be consistent to see desired results.

8. Whining

Barking, growling, and whining are all ways dogs communicate. A dog may be whining for a number of reasons, whether it wants something or is in pain.

However, you should be careful how you react to your dog's whining and try to understand the underlying cause. When a puppy is encouraged to whine, even unintentionally, this can lead to behavior that leads to excessive whining. It's possible to calm the whining and maybe even stop it by taking a few steps.

How to handle the behavior:

Before you try to address your dog's excessive whining, it's best to learn the reason why. While some people are fine with a little whining now and then, others can barely tolerate it and find it excessive and bothersome. You can train your puppy to whine less or to stop whining altogether.

- ❖ If your dog begins whining, you should pay close attention to any other behaviors that accompany it. Different reasons can cause whines to change their pitch and volume over time. You may become accustomed to whining like "I want something" or "I'm bored." Identifying whines that sound very different may help you to determine whether the whine is actually a result of stress or pain.
- ❖ If your dog seems stressed or pain-induced, approach it carefully and handle it gently. Otherwise, the whining can escalate and even turn aggressive.
- ❖ Consider the potential reasons for the whining objectively before deciding what to do. Never punish or yell at your dog for whining, as this can make a fearful or anxious dog even more anxious, which may lead to aggressive behavior.

- Try to find the source of the problem if your dog seems anxious, fearful, or otherwise stressed out. Dogs can suffer from a variety of fears and phobias. Identifying the cause may help you train and desensitize your dog to overcome its fear.
- If your dog wants something, give it what it wants. You shouldn't reinforce indoor elimination behaviors by leash-training your dog or allowing it to go outside when it's whining.
- Be careful not to encourage your dog to whine unintentionally. Before giving in to your dog's desire for attention or food, try redirecting him to another behavior. You should encourage your dog to sit or lie down quietly, then reward him or her with attention, praise, or a treat.
- Your dog will only whine more if you give in to its whims immediately. Problem whining is usually caused by giving in to the dog's whims instantly. Despite the fact that your puppy is whining, you might be left with an adult who's whiny.
- Make their environment more stimulating. Get them lots of toys, and make sure they exercise. Whining is more likely to occur in dogs with pent up physical or emotional energy.

❧ Be selective in how you respond to your dog's whining. You should ignore it if you're sure there's no need for it. When you notice a moment of silence, you can reward them with praise, treats, or something similar. It's also a great time to practice the "quiet" command.

9. Afraid of noise

Loud noises, such as fireworks or thunderstorms, can frighten dogs who suffer from noise anxiety. A dog may exhibit many anxious behaviors or even run away from home out of fear. Young children often run to their parents when they hear a scary noise at night. In response, most people say, "Don't worry, it's just thunder." Or, "No need to be concerned, it's just a noise."

No amount of reassuring or explaining will ease the anxiety of a dog afraid of noise. Noise anxiety affects millions of dogs across the nation. According to estimates, somewhere between 5 million and 15 million dogs suffer from severe enough noise anxiety that their owners seek help. There are options available to help your dog who's stressed by loud noises. Prior to attempting to remedy the problem on your own, you should consult your veterinarian for a proper diagnosis.

How to handle the behavior:

For professional diagnosis and treatment advice, you should consult your veterinarian before treating your dog for noise anxiety on your own. Dogs respond differently to various treatments. It's impossible to say which alternative will work the best for your dog. Ask your vet about safe alternatives. When evaluating which treatment may be the most effective, it's important to consider other factors as well. Some treatments take a great deal of time to administer. There are also risks associated with some treatments. Sometimes a dog's condition is best treated with a combination of treatments. The following options should be discussed with your veterinarian.

Change the Dog's Environment

There's a number of common sense, simple things you can do if feasible. If your dog exhibits anxiety, you can make the following changes to its environment:

Make your dog's crate a safe haven, or find an area where the noise level is reduced. To mask the sound of the problem noise, turn on soft music or the television. Exercise your dog before a storm or fireworks, for example, if you know one is coming. Doing so can burn off excess energy that could otherwise lead to anxiety. The above methods may not show dramatic results, but they can definitely reduce symptoms.

Pressure Wraps

Despite its simplicity, this is an effective and simple treatment for many dogs. "Pressure wraps" are wraps that provide constant, gentle pressure to the chest and torso of the dog. How do they work? It's not known for sure, but it's likely to be a combination of comforting the dog and distracting him or her from the fear.

A t-shirt of an appropriate size can be made into one, or else you can purchase a Thundershirt. Many dogs respond well to pressure wraps after their first usage, but some dogs require two, three, or more applications before you see improvements.

Behavior Modification

Noise anxiety is usually treated by desensitization. Start by exposing them to low levels of loud noise in a controlled environment. Over time, you can increase the volume louder and louder until they learn to tolerate the real thing. Talk to your veterinarian and possibly a professional pet behaviorist.

Medications

There are tons of medics available to your vet if your dog's anxiety is severe enough. These medications are administered regularly for the rest of the dog's life. Others are administered only when anxiety occurs. Ask your vet if there are any risks or side effects associated with the drugs you're considering. Sedating their dogs with over-the-counter medications such as Benadryl is common among pet parents. Don't do this without consulting a veterinarian first.

Pheromones & Supplements

Dog owners may opt for more natural remedies such as pheromones or supplements designed to calm dogs. There are many alternatives to medication that often cause fewer side effects.

There are a few products on the market that emit natural pheromones that can have a calming, reassuring effect on dogs. There are several different types of collars, diffusers, sprays, etc. Some dogs can also benefit from calming supplements in the form of chews, additives, or drops. Your veterinarian can provide recommendations.

10. Separation

Many dogs suffer from separation anxiety to varying degrees. During the first few weeks, a puppy might frequently bark for attention, but he or she might also suffer from serious, sustained separation anxiety. When left alone, dogs typically exhibit problematic separation anxiety.

Separation further usually causes dogs to follow you around and to bark and whine incessantly when you're not in sight. Besides drooling and panting, they may also try to escape from the confinement they're in (even if it causes physical harm to them), have more potty accidents than usual, and dig up or chew up things, even after you have adequately exercised them.

How to handle the behavior:

Don't expect to resolve this issue quickly—it can take some time, depending on the severity of the case. You can't fully cure your dog's anxiety, but you can help mitigate it. If your dog is experiencing significant distress, consult with your vet right away.

Here are some other things you can do:

- 🐾 Almost all types of anxiety in dogs are reduced by regular physical and mental exercise, just like in humans. Train your dog before you leave the house.
- 🐾 A good way to introduce the concept of separation to your dog is to have him or her relax in one's crate or puppy-proofed area while you are, say, cooking dinner. Slowly

increase the time by starting with a few minutes and working your way up.

* You want to keep your departures as low-key as possible. Whenever you go through your routine of getting your keys, putting on your shoes, etc., put your dog in a room or other area that he is comfortable in. He or she might not become overly nervous this way.

* Keeping him or her occupied while you are away might also help. Dogs can paw at or chew on toys that hold treats that come out when they bite or paw them. They're an excellent distraction.

* Don't yell or punish your dog for destroying your property, having potty accidents, or barking because it's stressed out. Avoid doing this at all costs.

* Many pet parents rush to a medication when their pets show signs of anxiety. If your dog appears overly anxious or harms himself or herself, talk to your veterinarian about whether or not this might be an appropriate treatment.

11. Aggression

Dogs that growl, snap, or bite regularly are likely to have serious behavior problems. Professional dog trainers or animal behaviorists are often sought out by dog owners due to aggression. All breeds are able to become aggressive when given the right conditions, not just large dogs and so-called "dangerous breeds."

Aggression can't be cured overnight, but you can take steps to curb aggressive behavior and calm your dog down.

How to handle the behavior:

You should keep a record of when your dog becomes aggressive and the circumstances surrounding the behavior. You'll need this information to decide what to do next. You must address the underlying causes of the aggression. Behavioral issues are symptoms of an underlying problem. You can calm the dog by managing the hostility in a number of ways. It will take time, consistency, and possibly professional assistance.

Consult Your Veterinarian

If your dog isn't typically aggressive but suddenly develops aggressive behavior, it might have an underlying medical issue. Among the health issues that can cause aggression are hypothyroidism, painful injuries, and neurological problems such as encephalitis, epilepsy, and brain tumors. Your dog may benefit from treatment or medication.

Engage a professional

A professional dog trainer or animal behaviorist should be consulted if your veterinarian has ruled out a medical issue. You shouldn't attempt to fix aggression on your own because it is such a serious problem. You can work with a professional to determine what causes your dog's aggression and create a plan for dealing with it.

Consult your veterinarian or the Association of Professional Dog Trainers for the name of a professional dog trainer or behaviorists.

Plan your strategy

Learn how to control dog's aggression by consulting with a behaviorist or trainer. The most common method of teaching your dog new behaviors is positive reinforcement.

You may want to start by standing far away from someone whom your dog doesn't know if he or she is mildly aggressive toward strangers. When you gradually decrease the distance between your dog and the stranger, reward your dog with treats and praise.

If your dog learns that strangers mean treats, you'll notice a reduction in its aggression. Using the same method, your dog can be accustomed to a variety of other situations as well.

Punishment should be avoided

When you punish your dog for aggressive behavior, the aggression usually escalates.

Whether you hit, yell, or use another aversive method, your dog may feel the need to defend itself by biting you.

As a result of punishment, your dog may also bite someone else without warning. Growling at children, for example, reveals that the dog is uneasy around them. Your dog may not warn you but may bite instead if you punish him or her for growling.

Medication may be required

There are times when training alone isn't sufficient. Some dogs that are aggressive may also require medication. During times of fear, stress, or anxiety, a dog cannot learn new things. If your dog is suffering from such anxiety, consider using medication to help. Medications are usually only needed temporarily for many dogs. Consult your veterinarian for more information.

Dealing with unavoidable situations

Lastly, make sure you can stick with your plan based on your lifestyle. It's nearly impossible to avoid a situation where a dog acts aggressively toward children if you have kids and the dog acts aggressively toward them. If this is the case, finding your dog a new home with only adults may be your best option.

CHAPTER 10

Step 4: Socialization

The best thing you can do for your dog is to socialize him or her, especially since socialization can greatly prevent behavioral problems down the road. Dogs begin socializing between six and 14 weeks of age, which is a critical time in their lives. This is when dogs are able to enjoy positive interactions with other dogs, people, noises, and activities, reducing their risk of fear and aggression later in life.

The most common reason dogs end up in shelters is because they aren't properly socialized. Dogs that aren't socialized properly are more likely to have behavioral problems. During those critical weeks, it's imperative that you expose your dog to a variety of animals, people, places, sounds, and experiences. Ensure that you do this throughout the entire first year your dog is with you. When you're out and about, bring your pet along with you and praise him whenever he's in a new situation or with someone or something new. If you give him or her a little meat or another treat, that will help teach tolerance. Don't be alarmed if you adopt a dog who's older than you are - I've seen that older dogs can benefit from socialization.

You will need to be patient, though, and it may take some time. There are no quick fixes for dogs that have had very little socialization and have deeply ingrained undesirable behaviors from it. Focus on steady progress over time rather than expecting dramatic results right away. It can take several months, or even years, to see drastic improvements on these issues. You should immediately remove your dog from the associated situations, animals, or people if your dog displays aggressive behaviors and you can learn more about aggression in the previous chapter. A positive association should be established when exposing your dog to new animals, people, or experiences.

Here's how you can do that:

Getting used to people

It's essential for your dog to be exposed to a wide variety of people, regardless of their age, size, or race, as well as those who look different in any way, including people in uniform, like a mailman, as well as those with a moustache or who use a walker. Put on a big hat and sunglasses and open an umbrella at a distance so as not to alarm your dog - these are all things he or she may find upsetting if s not used to them.

Ensure that your dog gets plenty of opportunities to meet men - dogs can be intimidated by men's large stature and deep voices. I recently worked with a dog named Smart, a rescue found by the side of the road as a stray. As soon as she met a new man, she became fearful, barked endlessly, and refused to approach him. It's likely that Smart's inability to socialize with men explains her behavior, regardless of any previous bad experiences she's had with them. During that first training session, my goal was to demonstrate to her that she could trust me. As soon as I started petting her and playing with her, she went from being wary of me and completely standoffish.

Obviously, a successful session doesn't mean Smart will be able to tolerate all men or even me on future visits - it generally takes weeks or even months for a dog to generalize like that. However, it was a start. By choosing people who will handle your pet gently, you can ensure that the fur baby will have a positive experience. Children can unintentionally be rough, so be careful around them. Bring good treats with you whenever you socialize your dog and encourage others to do the same. If your dog reacts well, have others pet him or her softly under the chin, not on top of the head. Petting one's chin reminds not to be scared of people.

Getting used to other dogs

Dogs shouldn't be the only ones on the block, so we should teach them that they're not the only ones. Throughout their lives, they'll encounter dogs of all kinds and sizes and must become comfortable with them, so they don't become fearful, aggressive, or both when they do. A lot of people think socialization is sufficient if their dog gets along with the neighbor's dog and the other dogs in the family.

Think about it from a human perspective: even if you get along with your best friend, siblings, and parents, it doesn't mean you'll be able to get along with everyone. It's likely that you'd behave differently when you encounter strangers if you only hung out with those people. Make sure you socialize him or her with friendly dogs.

It would be uncomfortable if your dog were confronted with another dog that lunged at him or attempted to bite him. Ask that person if that dog interacts well with others if you'd like your own dog to meet them. You may move on if the person seems hesitant or says anything other than "He loves other dogs!" politely move on. Try to avoid potential bad experiences whenever possible. Other dogs are available for you to play with. Don't let your dog run free in a dog park during this time. It is quite possible that he could encounter a not-so-friendly dog and end up having a negative experience. Dog parks are notorious for this. Moreover, make sure your puppy is around only healthy dogs who have been vaccinated, so he or she doesn't catch a serious illness.

When introducing your new pet to other dogs, follow the same guidelines that I described earlier in this chapter for when you introduce your new pet to the resident family pet. Observe the dogs' body language: if they are sniffing each other and wagging their tails, they are likely to want to play. Additionally, if one or both dogs are doing the "play bow"-crouching down on their front legs, butts raised-that's a universal dog greeting and usually indicates that things are going well. Nevertheless, if you notice that either dog is growling excessively, snapping, or if they have their tails between their legs and seem afraid or aggressive, find a new dog for yours to socialize with.

It's important to socialize your dog with other animals. Show him or her people on bikes, construction workers, and lawnmowers. Give your pup as many experiences, sights, and sounds as possible.

It's better to break new experiences into small steps for your dog, especially if he is apprehensive. For example, allow your dog to sniff the vacuum cleaner before turning it on! Wait a moment before turning it on. Whenever your dog seems frightened, you can take a step back and gradually increase the time the vacuum is on. Be sure to reward your dog along the way with treats and praise.

CHAPTER 11

Step 5: Commands, Tricks, & Games

Your first concern might be when to start training your dog once you've brought him or her home.

I'll tell you the facts.

You need to start right away!

It's fascinating to see what your puppy can learn at such a young age. Yet it's completely untrue that you can't teach an old dog new tricks if you have an older dog. Whatever your dog's age is, one will be eager to learn from you the minute the animal meets you. Canines crave human interaction to feel complete, as it's a natural instinct.

Training sessions can be divided into two categories: primary sessions, where you attempt to teach your dog a new skill, and secondary sessions when you allow your dog to learn on his or her own. However, you choose to train, keep these points in mind:

Don't expect unrealistically fast results

You'll find that your dog is able to learn some skills very quickly such as "sit;" however, others, such as ignoring distractions on a walk, can take a large amount of time. You'll achieve faster results if you move at a slower pace. Develop a rough draft of the behaviors you want to achieve for the first six to eight weeks. Your dog's behavior will then be appropriate for your family within six months to a year, at which time you can fine-tune it to align with your family's lifestyle, needs, and ultimate goals.

You won't have linear, successive progress

Some bumps will occur on the way to success, and that's natural. Have you ever learned a concept in class and believed you understood it? However, after you got home and had to do homework related to that concept, you didn't understand it at all? Many dogs feel the same way as well. Never blame your dog. Minimizing your mistakes will enable your pup to learn more quickly.

Dogs learn best after exercise

Having dogs that do not listen when introduced to new concepts is a big concern for many of my clients. Almost all dog owners don't exercise their hyper dogs before primary training because they don't realize that they need to do this. You need to burn off the excess energy in dogs like this in order to help them absorb new concepts. Prior to training your energetic dog, engage in a vigorous activity with her, such as fetch.

Be flexible!

When it comes to training your dog, things aren't always black and white. You should stop generalizing about your dog's breed or mix and start focusing on him or her as an individual.

GENERAL COMMANDS FOR BEGINNERS

No matter what learning stage your dog is currently in, you can teach it a few simple commands. In this section, I'll explain to you what all dogs should know about basic behavior.

Supplies Needed:

- ❧ Leash measuring four to six feet
- ❧ An eighteen to twenty-foot lead leash
- ❧ Harnesses or non-metal collars
- ❧ Incentives
- ❧ Some favorite toys
- ❧ An optional clicker

Watch Me (or Look at Me)

The fastest way to help train your dog to focus on you and listen to you no matter what's going on in the environment. In fact, it's the very first lesson to be taught to most dogs. It'll be more difficult to guide your dog if he or she isn't looking at you.

As with humans, eye contact is essential when communicating with your dog. My point here isn't to tell you to stare a dog in the eye you don't know. Some dogs might find that intimidating. The point is to learn to connect with your dog.

Here's what to do:

1. Consider sitting on the ground so that you are at eye level with your dog if this is comfortable for you. Offer your dog a treat directly before his eyes. Watch your dog as soon as you make eye contact with her. When your dog appears to be interested in the treat, say, "Watch me!" Close yourself in, keeping your training bubble small so you don't frighten your dog. Initially, target the pupils more likely to understand your wants if you're closer to her. Keep repeating this. If your dog reliably looks at your eyes when you hold the treat up, you can proceed to the next step.

2. Using your index finger, point to the eyes again without a treat in your hand, as most dogs are very receptive to body language. By doing this, your dog will look at your finger rather than the food. When he or she looks at you, say, "Watch me! And you can then reward her with another treat. Are you getting the picture? Here's our first-hand signal, and how powerful it is! Give this one lot of rewards for weeks upon weeks.

3. Become more confident about standing straight up by gradually stretching your training bubble. In order to gain control over your dog, you must be able to keep his or her attention for five or 10 seconds while standing up. You'll know when your dog is paying attention to you once she has her eyes on you!

Leave It

Having a dog ignore objects on the ground can save one's life if the pup is about to eat something she finds on the ground. "Leave it" will function as the foundation for distraction training (I'll cover it in a bit). Leaving anything alone can easily be taught to your dog without any human touch or restraint.

Here's what to do:

1. Take a tiny piece of treat in your hand. Hold it out to your dog. In the early stages, if your dog is energetic, she may try to reach it frantically, so keep your hand shut to prevent that at first. When a dog loses interest after 30 seconds or two minutes, you can reply, "Yes," and then after a pause of one half-second, you can answer, "Leave it," while giving him or her food. You can repeat this procedure several times.

2. Following that, you should offer your dog a small piece of food. Once again, he or she will probably lunge for it, so restrict access to the food by placing your hand over it and saying, "No." Since saying "No" always has consequences, in this case, the consequence is that he or she can't eat. You should avoid touching your dog, pulling him or her away from the food, or inadvertently pushing it backward. Rather than forcing the dog to leave the morsel alone, you're encouraging your dog to think for itself. This is a great example of "inside-out" education.

3. Let your dog slowly discover the food, covering it up each time he or she tries to get it prematurely. As soon as your dog isn't interested in it or is using even the smallest amount of self-restraint, firmly but enthusiastically say "Yes, leave it!" Then reward your dog. Give the food instead of allowing

the dog to eat it off the floor, so he or she understands that rewards always come directly from you. Continue doing this frequently.

4. Your dog will then be able to understand the concept of "leave it" and learn how to respond to real-life distractions with spontaneous training sessions of sixty seconds. Practice this as much as you can. Getting really good at "leave it" is required for setting up many future training sessions!

Leave It/Watch Me Combo

You've now mastered "leave it" and "watch me"; now let's consider combining them. Exercises such as this are somehow magical and are one of the most important lessons because they're the first steps in teaching your dog to listen to you even when distracted.

A mellow training session might teach your dog to leave something alone, but it's another matter to train her to do it while you're on a walk while encountering another dog, a cat, or a chicken bone. In the event you succeed in this exercise (which you will!), you'll be unstoppable!

Here's what to do:

1. Get started at home. Use a piece of meat to perform a "leave it" drill. Instead of seeing your dog walking away from the meat, tell him or her to watch you by saying, "Watch me." (Because the variable has changed, from leaving the meat to watching you), your dog may be confused at first, so don't expect a polished result immediately.) When he or she does, say, "Yes" and do well to reward it. What are you doing there? In essence, you're getting your dog's attention off the meat in front of it instead of on YOU! Dogs need to be able to do this before they are likely to listen to you at any time outside the house.

2. Switch up the routine a bit. Give the dog one of his favorite toys. Do the "leave it/watch me" drill again after dropping it? You should practice this as much as possible in a variety of ways. Toys and treats can be tossed by you to your dog as it walks, either away from it, towards it, or to the left or right of it. You're showing him or her how to act when faced with mild distractions at first, so that the pup can easily learn to deal with more serious distractions in the future.

3. The lesson can be moved to your front yard or driveway if you're doing well. At first, this significant difference may cause your dog some confusion, so be patient and don't demand that he

or she do the "leave it/watch me" drill as well as he or she did inside.

4. Your dog will learn how to look for you even if it's tempted by something desirable during this training exercise. Make sure to practice it in a variety of situations as your dog becomes more adept at it. For instance, let's say you notice another dog behind a fence across the street. In essence, the dog is now the distraction, rather than the treat or toy, as you practice "watch me" from a distance that isn't too overwhelming for it.

As with any skill, practicing it when your dog is really excited about looking, hearing, or smelling something will take time. Low-energy dogs are typically less persistent by nature, so they learn quickly. Nevertheless, if you have a high-energy dog as I do, try to get a lot of successes back to back (even if they are very small ones).

Sit/Down/Up/Stand

Multiple concepts can be learned simultaneously by dogs, so I often combine "sit," "down," "up," and "stand" in one lesson. The lure training technique is used to entice a dog to reach a specific position by using a treat. It isn't just throwing treats to your dog; in fact, it's actually using treats to direct him or her into the desired position. Rather than forcing your dog, you can show him what you want this way. This type of training is effective in many situations.

Using a treat and the dog's nose, not her eyes, is the most effective way to train a dog to follow a lure. Therefore, remember that the treat and the dog's nose are powerful magnets. Whenever you first lure the dog, keep the two as close together as possible. Dogs lose interest in the lure if the treat gets too far away from their nose. In addition, most people lure too quickly at the beginning. Take your time when luring. You'll get better results this way. You're likely not using the right treat for your dog. You're moving too fast or asking him or her to do something in an unfamiliar or distracting environment. The fur baby simply needs a bit more time to adjust.

Here's what to do:

❧ Sit

Ensure that your dog can see the treat that you're holding between your thumb and forefinger. While it's very close to your dog's nose, lift it just above the bridge of its nose, so that she or he can lift its nose directly upward toward the ceiling or the sky. A dog will usually naturally sit down once its head is tilted back. When your dog lands, say, "Yes, sit" one time, then provide a treat and some enthusiastic praise. (If she or he jumps up, you're putting the treat too far away from its face.)

❧ Down

Next, move the treat slowly down to the ground while your dog is seated. Keep the treat in front of its nose so that it follows the lure and goes down. You can say something like "Great job, you're down" and give her the treat after she lies down. In some cases, especially the smaller dogs, a lure cannot be followed well during a "down." In these instances, it may be essential to lure down and inward toward the chest area. You can also "capture" a down.

A lot of dogs turn in a circle prior to lying down, giving you an indication that they're getting ready for it. While your dog performs the action, you'll need to say "Down." As long as you're consistent, you'll still get there if you rely on capturing behaviors.

❧ Up

Raising the lure back up after "sit" and "down" will cause your dog to naturally reach for the lure. Since dogs are mostly obedient (though some might need a little bribery) to get treats, the lure can be placed farther away from their noses. In this case, you want her to return to the seated position. Using this technique, your dog will rise into a sit position when his or her head reaches up. When your dog reaches his or her head up and goes into a sit, say, "Yes, up," and reward him or her accordingly.

❧ Stand

Taking the lure out of your dog's face, move it slightly upwards. This will cause your dog to stand up naturally on all fours after it's has been in the sit position for a few seconds. Once the pup does this, say, "That's it!" Stand!" Let the dog have a reward. He or she deserves it! Don't wait too long to acknowledge your dog, since many of them will walk toward the treat after taking a step or two.

Stop your dog from being accustomed to this habit.

Of course, these four skills don't always have to be requested at the same time or in the same order. Make it interesting for your dog by mixing it up! I believe that this is one of the best ways to keep your dog interested and stimulated. You need to keep your timing extra tight if your dog is particularly energetic or wound up, because the moments of success will come rapidly. If you don't acknowledge the moment, you're also missing the opportunity to convey that you desire the moment to be repeated.

Once your dog has become comfortable sitting, lying down, etc., you can initiate a hand signal that's similar to the lure at first. You can then gradually change it into whatever hand signal is comfortable for your dog. You can get some traction with this process by faking your dog out a bit. This will enable you to have the treat in your other hand while you're actually holding the treat.

Just as he or she is getting into a certain position, start saying the words and using the hand motion. Once your pup gets into the position, give it the treat from the opposite hand. It shows your dog that you want it to watch your hand, not the treat when you give the pup a signal.

Come

All dogs should be able to learn this skill. Your dog should not run into danger only to ignore you when he or she hears you calling her. Teaching "come" as soon as possible should be a top priority.

Here's what you need to do:

- ☘ If possible, place your dog between you and a second person in a quiet, familiar environment. Whenever you teach "come" by yourself, keep your dog on a leash

- ☘ Be sure your dog is within a few feet of you when you begin. You'll find that your dog will learn quicker if you're close to him or her. Bring your dog to you by showing that you have a reward in hand and calling in an inviting and high-pitched tone of voice. You don't need to be modest! Your main goal is to make your dog as excited as possible.

- ☘ It's not just about making your dog come to you, but about making her really want to come to you. Praise him or her enthusiastically when one takes even one step toward you. Say, "Great! Come!" Your dog deserves a reward for this. You must make your dog understand that by coming to you, good things are going to happen to it. Make sure that your dog runs back and forth between you and the other person if you're working with another person.

- ❧ Gradually increasing the distance from which the dog should be called. Reduce the distance if your dog stops approaching you during training, then slowly try to get back to that point. During controlled training sessions, high-energy dogs tend to respond well to commands such as "come," whereas a more reserved dog may need a moment to process what's happening. When your dog isn't expecting it, for example, while you're cooking or working on your computer, practice this often. In this way, you'll encourage him or her to generalize the concept outside of the initial training sessions.

- ❧ Take your training sessions outside once you have succeeded repeatedly at home. Ensure that your dog is on a long leash to ensure that you're in control. You can entice most dogs to come by running away from them. Dogs love chasing after things, so make yours chase after you! Tell your pup, "Yes, please!" and give it a reward.

Over the next several months of training, prioritize taking your dog to lots of different places and practicing "come." I can't emphasize this too much, as this is how you'll teach your dog to generalize this skill in various environments. Just make sure to have your dog on a long lead leash.

Stay

Teaching "stay" can be broken down into three major categories: stay for a period of time, stay with distance, and most importantly, stay while distracted. The key is to break this down and add only one new variable at a time, so you don't overwhelm your dog.

Here's what to do:

❀ Stay for a Period of Time

During this process, keep your dog close by. Your pet will get excited to start training if you ask it to sit or lie down. If it sits or lies down, put your hand in front of the dog as if you were asking it to stop. Let it know exactly how to respond. Identify the smallest reason for an acknowledgment of a stay. Whenever he or she doesn't move, say, "Great!" Stay!" and reward him or her. Say "No" if the dog moves and then repeat the process.

Add a few seconds to your stay after you have mastered a brief stay. For example, you might start with one second, then two, then three. You could work up to 30 seconds. You should reward smaller moments more frequently at first if your dog is hyper, high-energy, as staying can be a great accomplishment for your fur baby. It may be possible to add time to your stay sooner than you expected if your dog is low energy. To avoid being too predictable, mix up the time periods you request along the way. Say "Okay" or "Release" after you've finished your dog's stay or whatever phrase you choose to convey the end of the stay. You must say "No" to your dog if it breaks its stay on any point, withhold the reward, and repeat the drill for a shorter period of time if it does so.

❧ Stay from a Distance

If you're on the ground and your dog is particularly clingy, as many puppies are, begin by moving just your head a few inches away. You can reward your dog for minor progress if he or she holds her stay. Get to the point where it can stand up while holding its stay. Again, reward your pup.

Add the distance now. Return promptly and reward your dog before she has a chance to move after taking a quarter-step backward. You aren't pausing yet at the end of your stay. In most cases, this is an intuitive action that can slow you down. It's better to alter one variable at a time.

Move one step back. Then, two steps back. Then, three steps back. Gradually increase your distance. You should immediately reward your dog when you've reached your desired distance. Trying too much of your dog too soon will cause her to fail two or three times in a row, so decrease the distance the next two or three times. This process shouldn't be rushed! It may require a few more training sessions for some dogs to reach five feet; other dogs may reach 55 feet during the first training session.

Once your dog is able to keep a distance for 20 to 30 repetitions in a row, and then add more time at different distances. Pause at this point. You're now combining distance and duration into one exercise which is quite amazing. Start by staying for a brief moment. Over the next week or two, try to reach 30 seconds.

Teaching Your Dog Proper Greetings

Whenever their dogs come home, many people enjoy it when they run to them and jump all over them. Even if you aren't entertaining guests or if your dog is large and can knock you over, it may not be a good idea to let your dog do that. If I ask my dogs to jump on me, I love it! In that sentence, the important part is that they're asked to greet me that way; otherwise, they won't do it without permission.

A dog's natural tendency is to jump on people when they see them. It's important, however, to teach your dog how to greet people properly. He or she can then jump as much as one likes, depending on how excited it is. Whenever you notice your dog is hyperactive and unable to focus on the lesson, let the dog run off some energy with a little exercise before beginning the lesson.

To get started, follow these steps:

1. At first, teach your dog how to greet you in your house when no other humans are around. When your dog jumps up for even a moment or shows he or she is about to, say "No" in a quiet voice and quickly step back. Stepping back so your dog

cannot physically interact with you, and not rewarding your dog, is the consequence in this case. For you to pay the dog any attention, it must have all paws on the ground! You can, however, praise and reward if the dog hesitates even for a split second and doesn't jump. In this way, it'll begin to realize that you'll pay attention to it if it doesn't jump. Plus, and if it doesn't jump, it'll receive a reward from you.

2. Next, set up training sessions that are more challenging. Try having your partner squeak a toy, or even having your friends encourage your dog to jump on them. A super-tempting exercise such as this has a lot of value because ultimately your dog should listen to you above all others. Even if guests say, "Oh, no problem," he or she shouldn't be allowed to jump on them at this point in training. Some guests may say, "No problem." In the end, it's your choice. Ultimately, it's up to you to decide whether or not jumping is appropriate. Unless you give permission, your dog must keep all four paws on the ground.

3. The first time your dog jumps at you, such as when you come home, just breathe, put your belongings down, and walk past your dog toward your treats. Make sure you have soft treats available at the front door. Reward your dog when it sits and stays. However, be a bit more reserved

than usual so as not to encourage excessive behavior. Try extending the time intervals over the coming weeks.

4. People make the mistake of assuming that their guests will do the steps I've described in this section when their dog jumps on them. The responsibility for teaching your pet proper manners lies with you. When you have company over, it's a good idea to keep your dog on a leash. This will ensure that you can keep him under control. And let your dog out to burn off some energy before having guests over if the pup is on a full battery. The dog might even stop jumping altogether if this is done.

If you're distracted, your dog won't learn not to jump on guests. To prevent your dog from jumping while entertaining your guest, tell them, "Excuse me; I have to spend the next 60 seconds training my dog not to jump." When he or she complies, allow the guest to pet your dog. You should create a human barrier between your dog and the person if he or she shows any signs of jumping.

You can also remove your dog from the setting if your dog is particularly hyper or untrained, or if you simply don't want to put much time and effort into training at the moment your guests arrive. If your guests enter your home for the first time, you may want to keep it in the bedroom. You can take the dog out on a leash, so you can pay more attention and focus once they're settled.

ADVANCED COMMANDS

It has been around since cavemen shared their bones with wolves in order to fetch, shake, speak, and play dead. Whether or not a dog has a title to its name, your pet is a top dog among your friends if it falls to the ground when hearing the word "bang" or when extending a polite paw when guests visit. Dogs are expected to learn these tricks, and it's your responsibility, perhaps even your duty, to teach them to your dog.

Many of these tricks have stood the test of time because they're simple to teach and easy to learn. Associating familiar actions with verbal cues allows them to capitalize on dogs' natural behavior. Do you have a vocal dog? Barking should be easy for you to elicit, associated with a cue, and rewarded. It's very likely that retrievers will start fetching before they reach adulthood. Hyper dogs will likely offer up their paws when "shaken." Let's begin learning these traditional favorites!

Shake Hands—Left and Right

Guests can shake the paw of your polite pooch by raising its paw to chest height when shaking hands. Both paws are taught this skill.

1. Hide a treat low to the ground in your right hand as you sit before your dog. When your dog raises the left paw, reward with a treat when you say "get it" and "shake."

2. Increase the height of your hand gradually until the dog is raising one's paw to chest height.

3. Make the switch to hand signals. While holding the treat behind your back with your left hand, extend your right hand while cuing "shake." When your dog paws your extended hand, reward it with the treat behind your back.

4. Teach "paw" on the opposite side by repeating these steps.

WHAT TO EXPECT:

It's an endearing gesture that any dog can learn. Make sure you practice twice a day, and always end on a high note. Combine these behaviors to create a quick succession of "shake" and "paw."

STEPS

1. Hold a treat low to the ground in your right hand.

2. Raise your hand when your dog gets better.

3. Cue your dog by standing up.

4. While you reward it, hold its paw.

Fetch/Take It

Your dog retrieves an object by being directed to do so. An example of this is when the fur baby puts something in its mouth that's within reach.

FETCH:

1. Slice a tennis ball in half with a box cutter to make a 1 in wide slit. Insert a treat into the ball and show your dog.
2. By patting your legs, acting excited, and running from the dog, you can encourage the dog to bring the ball back to you.
3. By squeezing the ball, you'll release the treat for your dog. Due to its inability to get the reward itself, the pup will learn to bring it to you.

TAKE IT:

1. When you give your dog the verbal cue, choose a favorite toy and playfully hand it to him her.
2. You can trade a treat for it after letting your pet hold it for a few seconds. Increase the time your dog holds the object before treating it as the dog improves. Don't treat your dog if it drops the toy on its own; you must remove it from its mouth.
3. Think outside the box! You can also have your dog carry a charming "feed me" sign as it circles the field. Seeing a dog holding a pipe or a basket of cocktail napkins is always amusing.

WHAT TO EXPECT

Several dogs are natural retrievers and will quickly learn this trick.

STEPS

Fetch

1. Make a slit in a tennis ball and drop a treat inside.

2. Toss the ball playfully.

3. Squeeze the ball to release the treat.

Take It

1. Hand your dog a favorite toy.

2. Trade him a treat for the toy.

3. Have your dog take and hold other objects!

Balance and Catch

At your signal, your dog catches a toy or treat, balances it on the nose, and throws it.

1. Your dog should be facing you in a sit. Put a treat on the bridge of your dog's nose while holding his or her muzzle parallel to the floor. Coach him or her to "wait" in a low voice.

2. Simply hold this position for a few seconds before releasing his muzzle and saying, "catch!" It's likely that exuberant dogs will send the treat flying. It's best to use a calm, quiet "catch" to slow down these dogs. Practice will help them become good at it.

3. When your dog allows the treat to fall to the ground, pretend to race him or her to pick it

up. The dog will learn to catch the treats or risk dropping them on the floor.

4. If your dog is improving, require him or her to balance the treat on his nose without you holding the muzzle. It's usually easiest to catch your dog's treat if you place it near the end of its nose, but each dog is different.

WHAT TO EXPECT

All dogs will benefit from the motor skills learned in this skill, even those with naturally better coordination.

STEPS

1. Hold the muzzle parallel and place a treat upon it.

2. Remove your hand while the pup balances the treat.

3. Practice will perfect your dog's catch!

Sit Pretty/Beg

You may have to beg if "please" doesn't work! Your dog keeps his or her rear on the floor while raising his forequarters from a sitting position. It's ideal for your dog to sit with a straight spine and paws tucked into his chest, on both hindquarters. In order to maintain balance, the pet's hindquarters, thorax, forequarters, and head must align.

Small Dogs

1. Your dog should be seated facing you in a sit position. Let him or her nibble the treat from your fist as you cue to "beg." When you want him to stay in this position, use a treat to lure the head up and back. Your treat should be lowered a little if he or she lifts one's hindquarters off the floor. Tell him or her to sit and tap one's bottom.

2. You can use verbal cues and hand signals as your dog's balance improve. Let your pup have the treat after several seconds. Don't reward your dog after he or she has lowered one's front paws; instead, reward while the pup is still standing correctly.

Big Dogs

1. Your dog should be seated in a sit position. Your heels should be together and your toes should be pointed apart as you stand directly behind it.

2. You can use a treat to help the dog to straighten up its head. Your other hand can hold its chest in place. Initially, the dog will need to find its balance; with improvement, use a lighter touch on its chest and back.

WHAT TO EXPECT

While some dogs learn to balance easily, others have much more difficulty doing so. Any dog can benefit from this trick since it strengthens the thighs and lower back. When you praise him or her, the fur baby will stand up and beg for more!

STEPS

Small Dogs

1. From a sit, lure his or her head up.

2. Allow it to nibble the treat.

3. As its balance improves, move away.

Big Dogs

1. Steady his or her chest while you lure the pup up.

2. Position your heels behind your dog, with your toes pointed apart.

COOL TRICKS

Who doesn't love cool tricks? Have you seen circus dogs!? Those puppies are cute!

I've compiled a list of cool tricks that you can teach your puppy.

Rollover

Dogs roll sideways on their backs during a full rotation. Start by putting your dog on his or her back, facing you. As you kneel down in front of it, hold a treat opposite the direction in which you want the pup to roll. When you tell your dog to "roll over," move the treat from its nose toward the shoulder blade.

This will encourage the dog to roll on its side. Give a treat and praise. As you move the treat from the shoulder blade toward the backbone, continue the motion with your hand. Ideally, this will entice him or her to roll over and go to the other side. Reward him or her after landing on its other side. You can use subtle hand signals to encourage as the pup improves. You can teach your dog to rollover in two weeks by practicing five to 10 times per session.

Play Dead

If your dog is playing dead, he or she will roll onto his back with its legs raised in the air. The pup then remains "dead" until you restore its life. Stick 'em up or you're a dead dog!

After you have given your dog some exercise and it has recovered from it, teach this trick. Put your dog down on its back and kneel in front of it. As you did when you taught how to roll over, hold a treat to the side of its head and move it toward the dog's shoulder blade. When your dog falls to his side, praise it. Help him or her to roll onto its back by gently guiding its midsection.

While lying on its back, give the pup a belly scratch and praise your pet. Say "good boy" as you do so. When your dog has been trained, just use the treat to get it into position without touching. In order to prevent the dog from rolling completely over instead of stopping halfway, hold his or her chest with your hand. Slowly release the grip so that it'll hold the position on his or her own. You should practice this skill until you can elicit the behavior using the "bang!" cue and hand signal. It's imperative that your dog stays in this position until told "OK" or "you're healed" or whatever the release word is.

Your dog might need a few days or weeks to get used to this position. Make sure you practice with your dog while rolling over.

Give Kisses

Dogs can be taught to kiss very easily. The wet doggie smooch isn't for everyone, but kids generally love this dog trick. Your dog will soon be able to reward you with all the desired attention on demand if you simply put a treat on your cheek and say the command. It's also beneficial to teach your dog to kiss on cue because you'll be able to prevent unwanted licking.

Wave

Want to teach your dog an intermediate trick? The "Wave" trick is perfect for you. Once you've mastered "give paw," have a treat ready and stand up facing your dog. Don't let your pup make contact with your hand.

After your dog has finished "giving paw," reward it with a treat and verbally mark them. Be sure your dog can wave without reaching for your hand as you practice!

Hug

If you want your dog to learn to give hugs, ask them to sit on a step or higher surface, or kneel down with your back facing the dog. To motivate your dog to get on your back, place a food lure on your shoulder and move your hand forward. Whenever your dog behaves well, reward it verbally and with treats. Work with your pup until he/she is able to come over your shoulder and into the hugging position, rewarding it proactively along the way.

Jump Hoop

Knowing how to train a dog is the first step to teaching your pet nearly anything-including how to jump through a hoop. When your dog walks through the hoop, reward him or her with a treat and a verbal cue each time. Simply encourage the pup to go through the hula hoop by putting it down on the ground. Keeping your pup's joints and bodily limits in mind, gradually raise the hoop off the ground as your dog understands. Your dog will soon be jumping through hoops, and you'll master the art of teaching an old dog new tricks!

CONCLUSION

Congrats! You made it to the end!

Your actions today will pay off in the future. I bet you!

Raising a dog isn't a walk in the park. If it were, we wouldn't be writing over 30 thousand words about how to get your dog to behave, would we?

As I said, the only thing better than a cute dog is an obedient one. No one wants an aggressive dog that goes around biting everyone and everything that comes its way.

There is no hard-and-fast rule to it when it comes to training dogs. I've highlighted several things in this book. But I should also add that your dog has a unique personality. Hence, not everything shared here might work on your dog. There's a real possibility that some dogs respond better to leash walking or cool tricks than others if you have more than one.

I once had a dog that hated going for walks. But when it comes to indoor mental dog games, that pup was excellent! I eventually got it a collar with a **"Dog Einstein"** nameplate.

In essence, you should always remember that training a dog is a responsibility. You ought to remain patient and committed to your dog's training process. Don't rush it.

If you're reading this book because you want to get a dog, then you should take chapter two more seriously. Understand the kind of dog breed that would suit you and know the best places to get them.

Following that, you should prepare your home, family, and mind to accommodate a new family member. Getting used to the whole family can be a slow and progressive for your new dog. So, give it time. Socializing might come naturally for some dogs. But for some others, it might take a while.

I should emphasize that you literally are all that your dog has! So, don't forget that your dog's health and grooming are of the utmost priority.

Getting into the core, there are tons of methods of training dogs. But in my decade-long experience, I've realized that positive reinforcement methods often yield the best results in the long run. With the proper knowledge and method, you can dutifully eliminate inappropriate dog traits such as urination, barking, and aggression, nausea in the car, eating feces, chewing things, jumping, digging, hyperactivity, whining, and much more.

There's an endless list of tricks and skills that a dog can learn in its lifetime. Don't put pressure on your dog to learn everything at once. That sort of pressure can lead to frustration for you and your dog.

I believe that if you put everything I've said in practice, you'll easily be able to bid your dog problems goodbye - as promised.

Here's my final takeaway for you:

While you might have family, friends, and colleagues, you truly are all your dog has! It needs attention, love, and patience. Treat your dog well, and it'll definitely reciprocate with obedience and love.

My best wishes to you on your doggy journey!

ABOUT THE AUTHOR

Born into a family of dog lovers, it didn't take much for Kory Baker to fall in love with canines. When you grow up tending to various breeds of dogs, it eventually grows on you. Kory Baker is a man in his 30s. He has always loved dogs and has been raising them since childhood.

What better way to culminate your love for dogs than to make a living out of it? Today, Kory works as a professional dog trainer for all kinds of dog owners and diverse dog breeds. He embodies the belief that those who love what they do will never 'work' a day in their lives. This has been his experience of working with various dog owners.

A proud owner of his dog training school, Kory has spent the last decades testing all kinds of training methods. He has put the best ones together into a detailed and convenient manual book, which is sold worldwide and is very popular among novice dog breeders.

LEAVE A REVIEW

Thank you so much for purchasing this book! You're truly one special dog owner, and your dog(s) is lucky to have someone as intentional and committed as you.

As an independent author with a small marketing budget, reviews are my livelihood on this platform. If you enjoyed this book, I'd really appreciate it if you left your honest feedback. You can do so by scanning the QR code below. I love hearing from my readers, and I personally read every single review.

REFERENCE PAGE

- ✓ https://www.thesprucepets.com/fun-and-easy-dog-tricks-1117309
- ✓ https://dogtime.com/reference/dog-training/34027-10-fun-impressive-tricks-can-teach-dog
- ✓ https://www.thesprucepets.com/dogs-and-aggression-1118229
- ✓ https://www.hillspet.com/dog-care/resources/picking-up-dog-poop
- ✓ https://dogtime.com/dog-health/dog-behavior/2580-noise-anxiety-dogs
- ✓ https://www.thesprucepets.com/why-dogs-whine-4147056
- ✓ https://www.cesarsway.com/6-steps-to-managing-a-dogs-over-excitement/
- ✓ https://www.cesarsway.com/how-to-calm-a-hyper-dog/
- ✓ https://pets.webmd.com/dogs/dogs-and-motion-sickness#1
- ✓ https://dogtime.com/puppies/1210-dunbar-object-aggression
- ✓ https://rawbistro.com/blogs/raw-bistro/food-aggression-in-dogs

- https://www.surepetcare.com/en-gb/advice-news/dog-care/dog-health-and-behaviour/why-rest-for-dogs-is-as-important-as-exercise
- https://wagwalking.com/training/use-a-litter-box-2
- https://pets.webmd.com/dogs/vomiting-dogs-causes-treatment#1
- https://www.k9ofmine.com/types-of-dog-training/
- https://pets.webmd.com/dogs/guide/dog-training-obedience-training-for-dogs#1
- https://dogtime.com/reference/dog-training/50743-7-popular-dog-training-methods
- https://pets.webmd.com/dogs/features/dog-training-positive-reinforcement-alpha-dog-method#1
- https://dogtime.com/dog-health/general/18529-10-ways-to-exercise-with-your-dog
- https://www.akc.org/expert-advice/health/how-much-exercise-does-dog-need/

Made in United States
North Haven, CT
29 April 2023

36051448R00134